Database Management Systems

P. Venkateswara Rao

Dr.A.P. Siva Kumar

Published by

BONFRING®
Intellectual Integrity

Database Management Systems

ISBN 978-93-92537-19-6

Authors

P. Venkateswara Rao

Dr.A.P. Siva Kumar

Bonfring

309, 5th Street Extension, Gandhipuram,
Coimbatore-641 012,
Tamil Nadu, India.
E-mail: info@bonfring.org
Website: www.bonfring.org

Acknowledgement

First of all, I am grateful to the Almighty God for establishing me to complete this text book.

My deepest gratitude to my supervisor, **Dr.A.P. Siva Kumar**, Associate Professor, Department of Computer Science and Engineering, JNTUA College of Engineering, Anantapuramu, Anantapur Dist, A.P.,. I have been amazingly fortunate to have a guide, who gave me the freedom to explore on my own and at the same time the guidance to recover, when my steps faltered. His patience and support helped me to overcome many crisis situations and finish this work.

I am thankful to management members of VNR Vigana Jyothi for their continuous support during this work.

I am thankful **to Dr.C.D. Naidu**, Principal, Deans and Directors of VNR Vignana Jyothi Institute of Engineering and Technology for their continuous support throughout my research work. I thank my HOD, CSE, **Dr.S. Nagini** and my Professors Dr.B.V. Kiranmayee, Dr.C. Kiranmai and Dr.T. Sunil Kumar who always support and guide me towards the completion of the research work.

I sincerely thank all my other colleagues of the Department of CSE for their helping hand.

I would like to thank my parents Sri. P Chennakesavulu, Smt. P. Koteswari and other family members who have been a source of strength and encouragement which helped me a lot at all stages of writing this books.

My heart felt special thanks to my wife **Smt. B. Naga Silpa,** Senior Software Engineer, Sons P. Suhas, and P. Srihaas, they always encouraged me and extended their unconditional and unstinting support.

This book is dedicated to all my family members. I thank the almighty for his blessings to complete this work.

Venkateswara Rao Pulipati

TABLE OF CONTENTS

CHAPTER 1

1. Introduction to Database Design and Relational Model

1.1. Database System Applications

Data: Data is meaningful known raw facts that can be processed and stored as information.

Database: Database is a collection of interrelated and organized data. In general, it is a collection of files (tables).

DBMS contains information about a particular enterprise.

- Collection of interrelated data.

- Set of programs to access the data.

- An environment that is both *convenient* and *efficient* to use.

Database Applications

- *Banking:* All transactions.

- *Airlines:* Reservations, schedules.

- *Universities:* Registration, grades.

- *Sales:* Customers, products, purchases.

- *Online retailers:* Order tracking, customized recommendations.

- *Manufacturing:* Production, inventory, orders, supply chain.

- *Human resources:* Employee records, salaries, tax deductions.

- *Databases:* Touch all aspects of our lives.

What is a DBMS?

- A very large, integrated collection of data.

- Models real-world enterprise. Entities (e.g., students, courses) Relationships (e.g., Madonna is taking CS564).

- A Database Management System (DBMS) is a software package designed to store and manages databases.

Why Use a DBMS?

- Data independence and efficient access.
- Reduced application development time.

1.2. Purpose of Database Systems

In the early days, database applications were built directly on top of file systems. Drawbacks of using file systems to store data:

- Data redundancy and inconsistency.
- Multiple file formats, duplication of information in different files.
- Difficulty in accessing data.
- Need to write a new program to carry out each new task.
- Data isolation — multiple files and formats.
- Integrity problems.
- Hard to add new constraints or change existing ones.
- Atomicity of updates.
- Failures may leave database in an inconsistent state with partial updates carried out.
  - *Example:* Transfer of funds from one account to another should either complete or not happen at all.
- Concurrent access by multiple users.
- Concurrent accessed needed for performance.
- Uncontrolled concurrent accesses can lead to inconsistencies.
  - *Example:* Two people reading a balance and updating it at the same time.
- Security problems.
- Hard to provide user access to some, but not all, data.
- Database systems offer solutions to all the above problems.

Advantages of DBMS

- **Data independence:** Provides an abstract view of the data that hides the details data representation and storage.
- **Efficient Data Access:** This is the advantage where we use variety of techniques to store and retrieve data.
- **Data integrity and security:** We can ensure data integrity if the data is always enforced through integrity constraint.

- **Data administration:** "Data" administration deals with the modeling of the data and treats data as an organizational resource, while "database" administration deals with the implementation of the types of databases that are in use.

- **Concurrent Access and crash recovery:** It ensures concurrent access of the data in such a way that the data is being accessed by only one user a time. Also protects the system from crashes.

- **Reduced Application Development time:** It supports all the important functions that are common to many applications.

Disadvantages of a DBMS

The following are disadvantages of DBMS.

- Setup of the database system requires more knowledge, money, skills, and time.
- The complexity of the database may result in poor performance.

1.3.   View of Data

- Data Abstraction.
- Instances and Schema.
- Data Models.

Physical Level

The lowest level of abstraction describes how a system actually stores data. The physical level describes complex low-level data structures indetail.

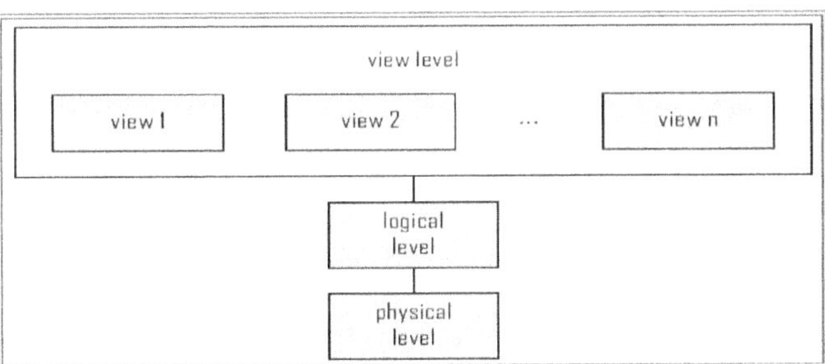

Logical Level

The next higher level of abstraction describes what data the database stores, and what relationships exist among those data. The logical level thus describes an entire database in terms of a small number of relatively simple structures. Although implementation of the simple structures at the logical level may involve complex physical level structures, the user of the logical level does not need to be aware of this complexity. This referred to as physical data independence. Database administrators, who must decide what information to keep in a database, use the logical level of abstraction.

View Level

The highest level of abstraction describes only part of the entire database. Even though the logical level uses simpler structures, complexity remains because of the variety of information stored in a large database. Many users of a database system do not need all this information; instead, they need to access only a part of the database. The view level of abstraction exists to simplify their interaction with the system. The system may provide many views for the same database.

1.4.   Instances and Schema

What are Instances?

The environment of database is said to be instance. A database instance or an 'instance' is made up of the background processes needed by the database software. These processes usually include a process monitor, session monitor, lock monitor, etc. They will vary from database vendor to database vendor. A database instance (Server) is a set of memory structure and background processes that access a set of database files.

What are Schemas?

A database schema of a database system is its structure described in a formal language supported by the database management system (DBMS) and refers to the organization of data as a blueprint of how a database is constructed.

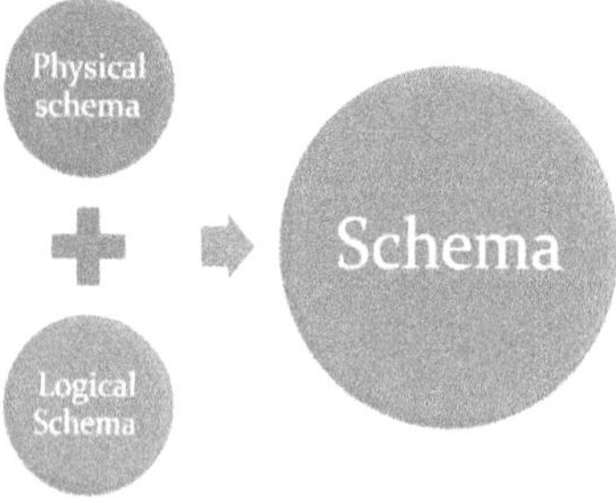

Physical Schema

- A physical data model (or database design) is a representation of a data design which takes into account the facilities and constraints of a given database management system.
- A physical schema is hidden beneath the logical schema, and can usually be changed easily without affecting application programs.

Logical Schema

A logical schema is a data model of a specific problem domain expressed in terms of a particular data management technology.

1.5. Data Models

Underlying the structure of a database is the data model: a collection of conceptual tools for describing data, data relationships, data semantics and consistency constraints.

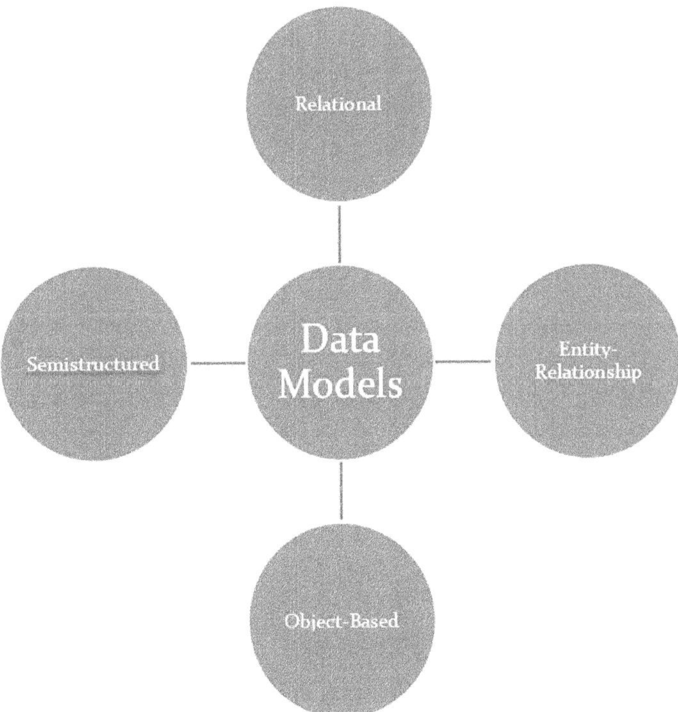

Relational Model

The purpose of the relational model is to provide a declarative method for specifying data and queries: users directly state what information the database contains and what information they want from it, and let the database management system software take care of describing data structures for storing the data and retrieval procedures for answering queries.

Entity - Relationship Model

An entity–relationship model (ER model) is a data model for describing the data or information aspects of a business domain or its process requirements, in an abstract way that lends itself to ultimately being implemented in a database such as a relational database. The main components of ER models are entities (things) and the relationships that can exist among them. Entity–relationship modeling was developed by Peter Chen.

Object - based Data Model

Object-oriented database management systems allow object-oriented programmers to develop the product, store them as objects, and replicate or modify existing objects to make new objects within the OODBMS. Because the database is integrated with the programming language, the programmer can maintain consistency within one environment, in that both the OODBMS and the programming language will use the same model of representation. Relational DBMS projects, by way of contrast, maintain a clearer division between the database model and the application.

Semi-Structured Data Model

The semi-structured model is a database model where there is no separation between the data and the schema, and the amount of structure used depends on the purpose. This is in contrast to the data models mentioned earlier where every data item of a particular type must have the same set of attributes.

Eg: XML

- A *data model* is a collection of concepts for describing data.
- A *schema* is a description of a particular collection of data, using the a given data model.
- The *relational model of data* is the most widely used model today.

Main concept: *relation,* basically a table with rows and columns.

Every relation has a *schema,* which describes the columns, or fields.

Example: University Database Conceptual Schema

Students (sid: string, name: string, login: string, age: integer, gpa: real) Courses (cid: string, cname: string, credits: integer).

Enrolled (sid: string, cid: string, grade: string).

Physical Schema

Relations stored as unordered files. Index on first column of Students. External Schema (View): Course_info (cid:string, enrollment:integer).

Data Independence

Applications insulated from how data is structured and stored.

- **Logical data independence**: Protection from changes in *logical* structure of data.
- **Physical data independence:** Protection from changes in *physical* structure of data.

1.6.   Database Languages

DDL (Data Definition Language): DDL or Data Definition Language actually consists of the SQL commands that can be used to define the database schema. It simply deals with descriptions of the database schema and is used to create and modify the structure of database objects in database.

Examples of DDL commands:

- **CREATE –** is used to create the database or its objects (like table, index, function, views, store procedure and triggers).

The general syntax for the create command in Data Definition Language is mentioned below:

CREATE TABLE table_name (Column1 DATATYPE, Column2 DATATYPE, Column3 DATATYPE, …….. ColumnN DATATYPE)

For Example

CREATE TABLE PUPIL (PUPIL_ID CHAR (10), STUDENT_Name CHAR (10);

- **DROP –** is used to delete objects from the database.

The General syntax of the Drop command is mentioned below:

DROP TABLE table_name;

DROP DATABASE database_name;

DROP TABLE Student;

DROP TABLE index_name;

- **ALTER** – is used to alter the structure of the database.

   The general syntax of the ALTER command is mentioned below:

   ALTER TABLE table_name ADD column_name (for adding a new column)

   ALTER TABLE table name RENAME To new_table_name (for renaming a table)

   ALTER TABLE table_name MODIFY column_name data type (for modifying a column)

   ALTER TABLE table_name DROP COLUMN column_name (for deleting a column)

For Example

Add column to the pupil table.

ALTER TABLE PUPIL ADD PHONE NUMBER varchar 97

Before Adding Column

Pupil ID	PUPIL_Name
97	Albert
98	Sameer

After Adding Column

PUPIL_ID	STUDENT_NAME	MOBILE NUMBER
97	ALBERT	
98	SAMEER	

- **TRUNCATE** – is used to remove all records from a table, including all spaces allocated for the records are removed.

   The syntax of the Truncate command is mentioned below:

   TRUNCATE TABLE table_name;

   TRUNCATE TABLE Student;

- **COMMENT** – is used to add comments to the data dictionary.

- **RENAME** – is used to rename an object existing in the database.

DML (Data Manipulation Language): The SQL commands that deals with the manipulation of data present in database belong to DML or Data Manipulation Language and this includes most of the SQL statements.

Examples of DML

- **SELECT** – is used to retrieve data from the a database.

For Example

Select author_name from book_set Where age> 40.

The names of the authors will be yielded by the command from the relation book_set whose age is greater than 40.

- **INSERT –** is used to insert data into a table.

Insert into Table_Name (column1, column2, column3..... columnN) Values (value1, value2, value3..... valueN)

For Example

Consider a table **Pupil** with the following fields.

P_id	P_Name	age

Insert into Student Values (78,'Nicole', 8).

The above command will insert a record into Pupil table.

P_id	P_Name	Age
78	Nicole	8

- **UPDATE –** is used to update existing data within a table.

The values of columns in a table can be modified or updated by using this command. The general syntax for this command is mentioned below:

Update table name

Set column_name1 = value1

column_name2= value2

column_name3= value3

...

Column_nameN= valueN,

(Where Condition)

For Example

UPDATE tutorialspoint SET Author= "webmaster" Where Author= "anonymous"

- **DELETE –** is used to delete records from a database table.

DELETE FROM table_name (Where Condition);

For Example

Consider the following Pupil Table.

P_id	P_Name	Age
78	Nicole	8
79	Ananya	11
80	Anu	9

Delete from Pupil where P_id=80.

The above-mentioned command will delete the record where P_id is 80 from Pupil Table.

P_id	P_Name	Age
78	Nicole	8
79	Ananya	11

1.7.   Relational Databases

RDBMS stands for **R**elational **D**atabase **M**anagement **S**ystem. RDBMS is the basis for SQL, and for all modern database systems like MS SQL Server, IBM DB2, Oracle, MySQL, and Microsoft Access.

A Relational database management system (RDBMS) is a database management system (DBMS) that is based on the relational model as introduced by E. F. Codd.

The data in an RDBMS is stored in database objects which are called as **tables**. This table is basically a collection of related data entries and it consists of numerous columns and rows.

Remember, a table is the most common and simplest form of data storage in a relational database. The following program is an example of a CUSTOMERS table:

```
+----+----------+-----+-----------+----------+
| ID | NAME | AGE | ADDRESS | SALARY |
+----+----------+-----+-----------+----------+
| 1 | Ramesh | 32 | Ahmedabad | 2000.00 |
| 2 | Khilan | 25 | Delhi | 1500.00 |
| 3 | kaushik | 23 | Kota | 2000.00 |
| 4 | Chaitali | 25 | Mumbai | 6500.00 |
| 5 | Hardik | 27 | Bhopal | 8500.00 |
| 6 | Komal | 22 | MP | 4500.00 |
| 7 | Muffy | 24 | Indore | 10000.00 |
+----+----------+-----+-----------+----------+
```

Every table is broken up into smaller entities called fields. The fields in the CUSTOMERS table consist of ID, NAME, AGE, ADDRESS and SALARY.

A field is a column in a table that is designed to maintain specific information about every record in the table.

A record is also called as a row of data is each individual entry that exists in a table. For example, there are 7 records in the above CUSTOMERS table. Following is a single row of data or record in the CUSTOMERS table:

```
+----+----------+-----+-----------+---------+
| 1 | Ramesh | 32 | Ahmedabad | 2000.00 |
+----+----------+-----+-----------+---------+
```

A record is a horizontal entity in a table.

A column is a vertical entity in a table that contains all information associated with a specific field in a table.

For example, a column in the CUSTOMERS table is ADDRESS, which represents location description and would be as shown below.

```
+-----------+
| ADDRESS |
+-----------+
| Ahmedabad |
| Delhi |
| Kota |
| Mumbai |
| Bhopal |
| MP |
| Indore |
+----+------
```

A NULL value in a table is a value in a field that appears to be blank, which means a field with a NULL value is a field with no value.

It is very important to understand that a NULL value is different than a zero value or a field that contains spaces. A field with a NULL value is the one that has been left blank during a record creation.

1.8. SQL Constraints

Constraints are the rules enforced on data columns on a table. These are used to limit the type of data that can go into a table. This ensures the accuracy and reliability of the data in the database.

Constraints can either be column level or table level. Column level constraints are applied only to one column whereas, table level constraints are applied to the entire table.

Following are some of the most commonly used constraints available in SQL.

- **NOT NULL Constraint** – Ensures that a column cannot have a NULL value.
- **DEFAULT Constraint** – Provides a default value for a column when none is specified.
- **UNIQUE Constraint** – Ensures that all the values in a column are different.
- **PRIMARY Key** – Uniquely identifies each row/record in a database table.
- **FOREIGN Key** – Uniquely identifies a row/record in any another database table.
- **CHECK Constraint** – The CHECK constraint ensures that all values in a column satisfy certain conditions.
- **INDEX** – Used to create and retrieve data from the database very quickly.

1.9. Data Integrity

The following categories of data integrity exist with each RDBMS:

- **Entity Integrity:** There are no duplicate rows in a table.
- **Domain Integrity:** Enforces valid entries for a given column by restricting the type, the format, or the range of values.
- **Referential integrity:** Rows cannot be deleted, which are used by other records.
- **User-Defined Integrity:** Enforces some specific business rules that do not fall into entity, domain or referential integrity.

1.10. Database Design

The ER model defines the conceptual view of a database. It works around real-world entities and the associations among them. At view level, the ER model is considered a good option for designing databases.

Entity

An entity can be a real-world object, either animate or inanimate, that can be easily identifiable. For example, in a school database, students, teachers, classes, and courses offered can be considered as entities. All these entities have some attributes or properties that give them their identity.

An entity set is a collection of similar types of entities. An entity set may contain entities with attribute sharing similar values. For example, a Students set may contain all the students of a school; likewise a Teachers set may contain all the teachers of a school from all faculties. Entity sets need not be disjoint.

Attributes

Entities are represented by means of their properties, called attributes. All attributes have values. For example, a student entity may have name, class, and age as attributes.

There exists a domain or range of values that can be assigned to attributes. For example, a student's name cannot be a numeric value. It has to be alphabetic. A student's age cannot be negative, etc.

Types of Attributes

- **Simple attribute –** Simple attributes are atomic values, which cannot be divided further. For example, a student's phone number is an atomic value of 10 digits.

- **Composite attribute –** Composite attributes are made of more than one simple attribute. For example, a student's complete name may have first_name and last_name.

- **Derived attribute –** Derived attributes are the attributes that do not exist in the physical database, but their values are derived from other attributes present in the database. For example, average_salary in a department should not be saved directly in the database, instead it can be derived. For another example, age can be derived from data_of_birth.

- **Single-value attribute –** Single-value attributes contain single value. For example – Social_Security_Number.

- **Multi-value attribute –** Multi-value attributes may contain more than one values. For example, a person can have more than one phone number, email_address, etc.

These attribute types can come together in a way like:

- Simple single-valued attributes
- Simple multi-valued attributes
- Composite single-valued attributes
- Composite multi-valued attributes

Entity-Set and Keys

Key is an attribute or collection of attributes that uniquely identifies an entity among entity set.

For example, the roll_number of a student makes him/her identifiable among students.

- **Super Key:** A set of attributes (one or more) that collectively identifies an entity in an entity set.
- **Candidate Key:** A minimal super key is called a candidate key. An entity set may have more than one candidate key.
- **Primary Key:** A primary key is one of the candidate keys chosen by the database designer to uniquely identify the entity set.

Relationship

The association among entities is called a relationship. For example, an employee **works_at** a department, a student **enrolls** in a course. Here, Works_at and Enrolls are called relationships.

Relationship Set

A set of relationships of similar type is called a relationship set. Like entities, a relationship too can have attributes. These attributes are called **descriptive attributes**.

Degree of Relationship

The number of participating entities in a relationship defines the degree of the relationship.

- Binary = degree 2
- Ternary = degree 3
- n-ary = degree

1.11. Mapping Cardinalities

Cardinality defines the number of entities in one entity set, which can be associated with the number of entities of other set via relationship set.

- **One-to-one:** One entity from entity set A can be associated with at most one entity of entity set B and vice versa.

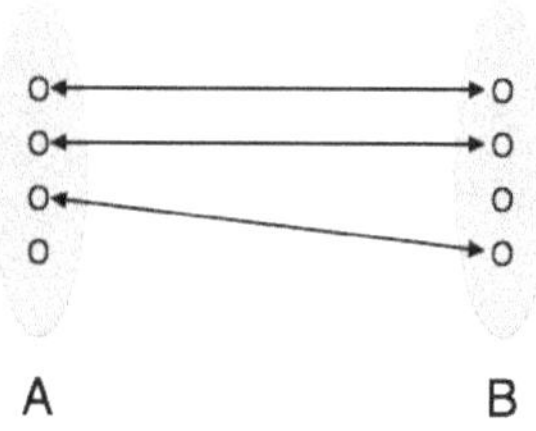

- **One-to-many:** One entity from entity set A can be associated with more than one entities of entity set B however an entity from entity set B, can be associated with at most one entity.

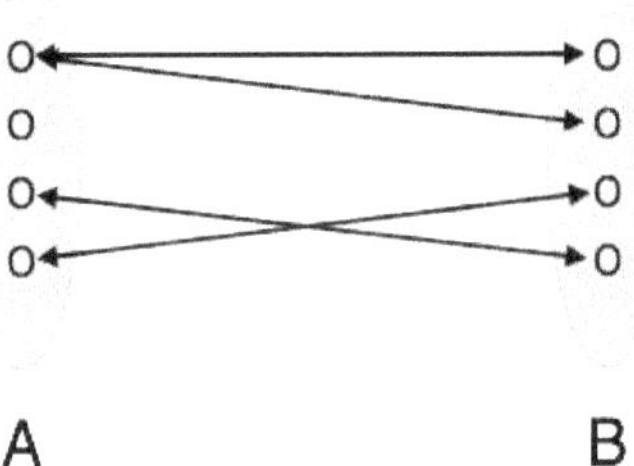

- **Many-to-one:** More than one entities from entity set A can be associated with at most one entity of entity set B, however an entity from entity set B can be associated with more than one entity from entity set A.

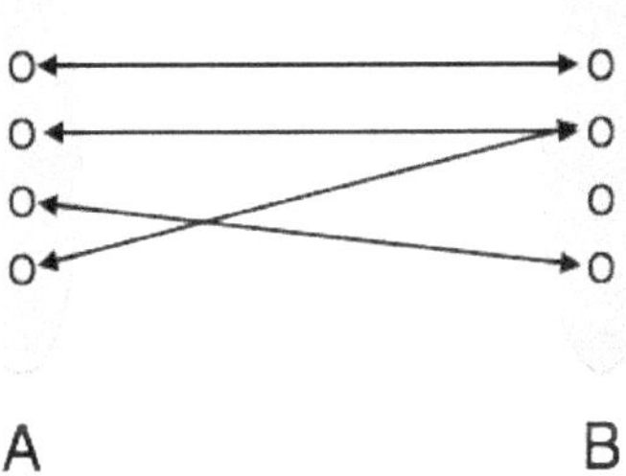

- **Many-to-many:** One entity from A can be associated with more than one entity from B and vice versa.

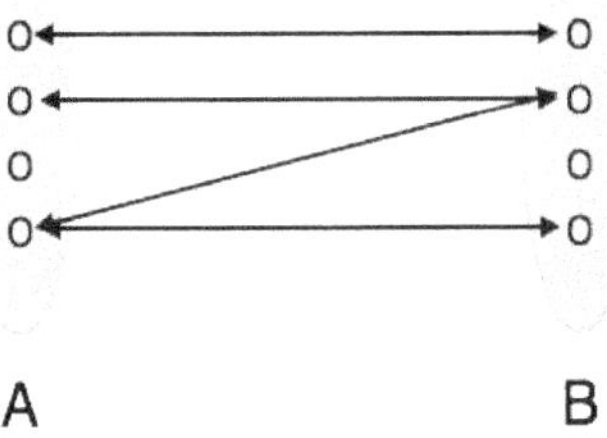

Entity

Entities are represented by means of rectangles. Rectangles are named with the entity set they represent.

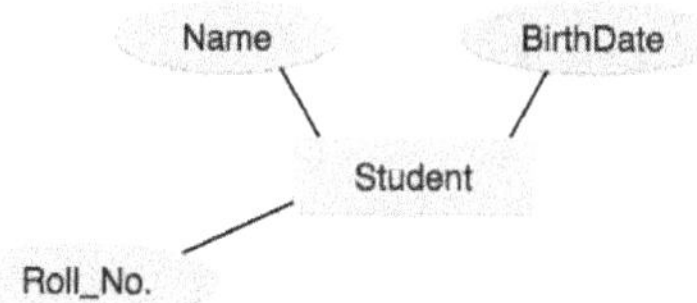

If the attributes are **composite**, they are further divided in a tree like structure. Every node is then connected to its attribute. That is, composite attributes are represented by ellipses that are connected with an ellipse.

Attributes

Attributes are the properties of entities. Attributes are represented by means of ellipses. Every ellipse represents one attribute and is directly connected to its entity (rectangle).

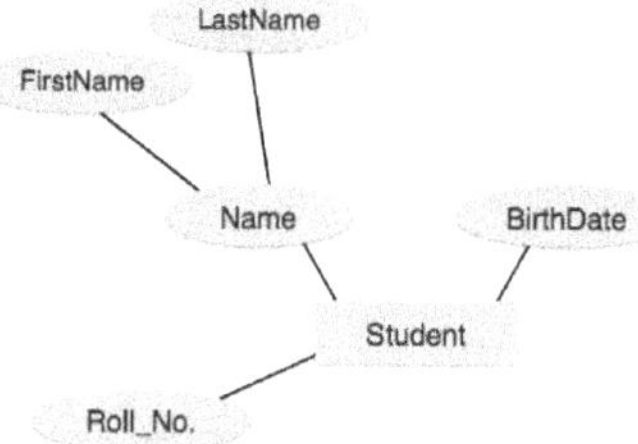

Multivalued attributes are depicted by double ellipse.

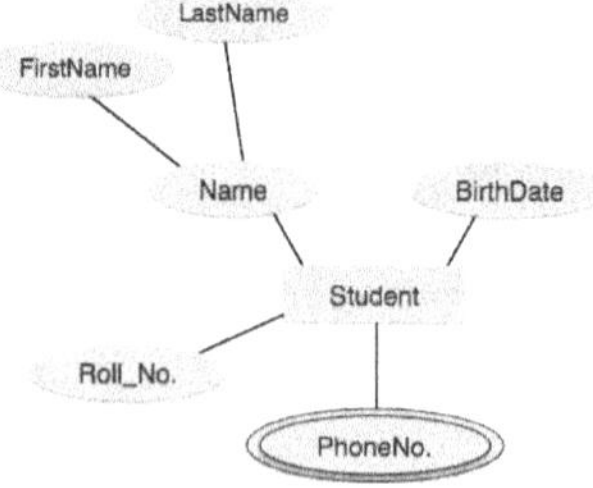

Derived attributes are depicted by dashed ellipse.

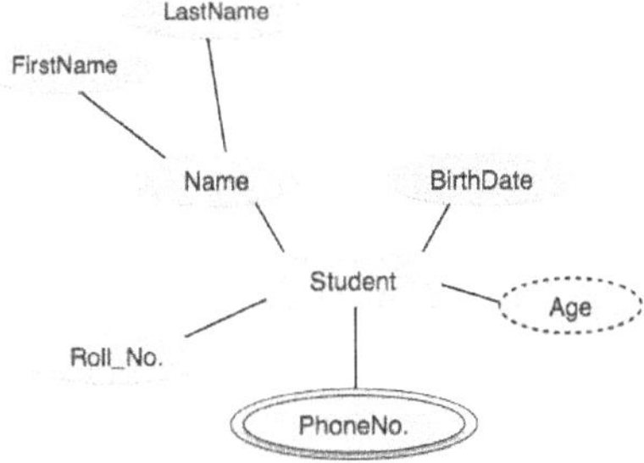

Relationship

Relationships are represented by diamond-shaped box. Name of the relationship is written inside the diamond-box. All the entities (rectangles) participating in a relationship, are connected to it by a line.

Binary Relationship and Cardinality

A relationship where two entities are participating is called a **binary relationship**. Cardinality is the number of instance of an entity from a relation that can be associated with the relation.

- **One-to-one:** When only one instance of an entity is associated with the relationship, it is marked as '1:1'. The following image reflects that only one instance of each entity should be associated with the relationship. It depicts one-to-one relationship.

- **One-to-many:** When more than one instance of an entity is associated with a relationship, it is marked as '1:N'. The following image reflects that only one instance of entity on the left and more than one instance of an entity on the right can be associated with the relationship. It depicts one-to-many relationship.

- **Many-to-one:** When more than one instance of entity is associated with the relationship, it is marked as 'N:1'. The following image reflects that more than one instance of an entity on the left and only one instance of an entity on the right can be associated with the relationship. It depicts many-to-one relationship.

Entity —— N —— Relationship —— 1 —— Entity

- **Many-to-many:** The following image reflects that more than one instance of an entity on the left and more than one instance of an entity on the right can be associated with the relationship. It depicts many-to-many relationship.

Data Storage and Querying

- Storage management.
- Query processing.
- Transaction processing.

Storage Management

- Storage manager is a program module that provides the interface between the low-level data stored in the database and the application programs and queries submitted to the system.
- The storage manager is responsible to the following tasks:
  - Interaction with the file manager.
  - Efficient storing, retrieving and updating of data.
- Issues:
  - Storage access.
  - File organization.
  - Indexing and hashing.

Query Processing

- Parsing and translation.
- Optimization.
- Evaluation.

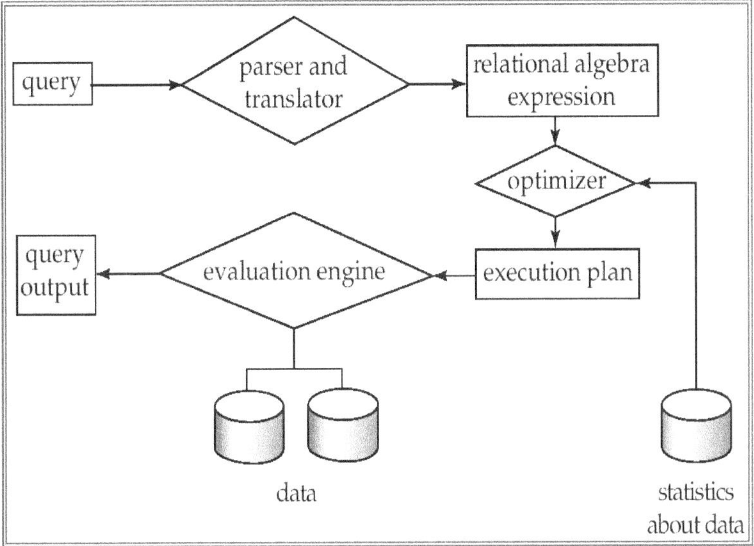

- Alternative ways of evaluating a given query.
    - Equivalent expressions.
    - Different algorithms for each operation.
- Cost difference between a good and a bad way of evaluating a query can be enormous.
- Need to estimate the cost of operations.
    - Depends critically on statistical information about relations which the database must maintain.
    - Need to estimate statistics for intermediate results to compute cost of complex expressions.

Database Architecture

The architecture of database systems is greatly influenced by the underlying computer system on which the database is running:

- Centralized.
- Client-server.
- Parallel (multiple processors and disks).
- Distributed.

Overall System Structure

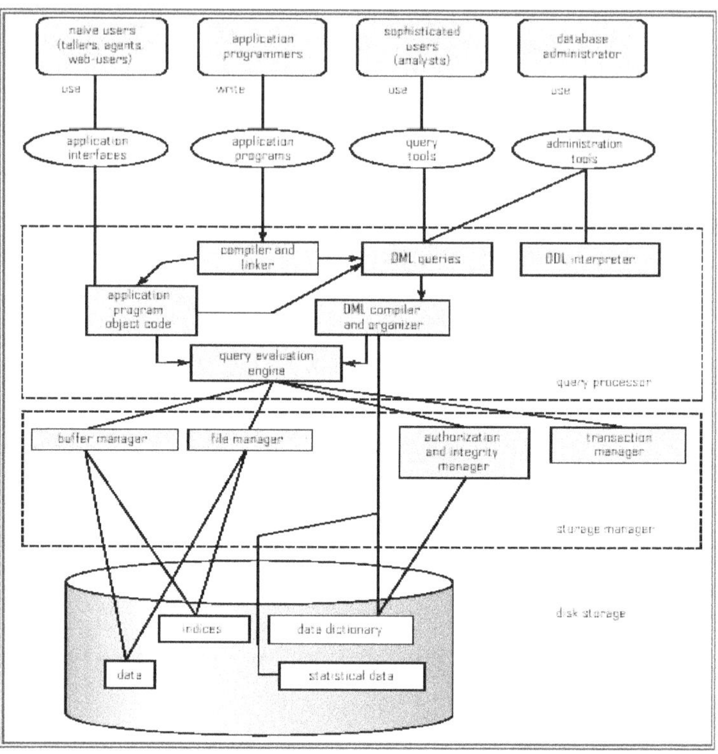

Database Application Architectures

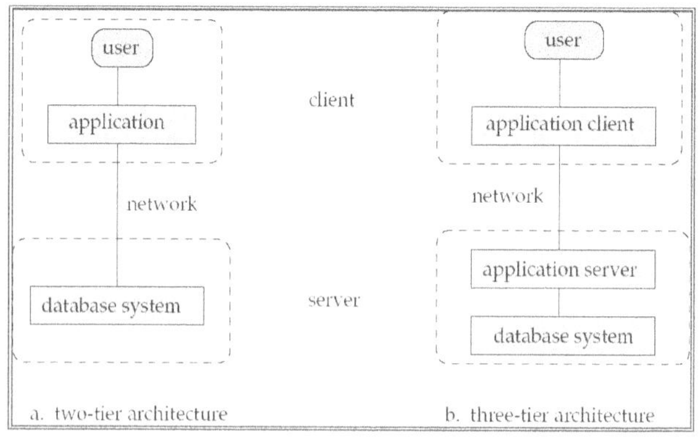

2-tier DBMS architecture includes an **Application layer** between the user and the DBMS, which is responsible to communicate the user's request to the database management system and then send the response from the DBMS to the user.

An application interface known as **ODBC** (Open Database Connectivity) provides an API that allow client side program to call the DBMS. Most DBMS vendors provide ODBC drivers for their DBMS.

3-tier DBMS architecture is the most commonly used architecture for web applications.

It is an extension of the 2-tier architecture. In the 2-tier architecture, we have an application layer which can be accessed programatically to perform various operations on the DBMS. The application generally understands the Database Access Language and processes end users requests to the DBMS.

In 3-tier architecture, an additional Presentation or GUI Layer is added, which provides a graphical user interface for the End user to interact with the DBMS.

For the end user, the GUI layer is the Database System, and the end user has no idea about the application layer and the DBMS system.

Data Mining and Information Retrieval

Data mining is looking for hidden, valid, and potentially useful patterns in huge data sets. Data Mining is all about discovering unsuspected / previously unknown relationships amongst the data.

It is a multi-disciplinary skill that uses machine learning, statistics, AI and database technology.

The insights derived via Data Mining can be used for marketing, fraud detection, and scientific discovery, etc.

Data mining is also called as Knowledge discovery, Knowledge extraction, data/pattern analysis, information harvesting, etc.

Data mining can be performed on following types of data.

- Relational databases.
- Data warehouses.
- Advanced DB and information repositories.
- Object-oriented and object-relational databases.

- Transactional and Spatial databases.

- Heterogeneous and legacy databases.

- Multimedia and streaming database.

- Text databases.

- Text mining and Web mining.

Data Mining Implementation Process

Business Under standing | Data Understanding | Data Preparation | Modeling | Evalution | Deployment

Business Understanding

In this phase, business and data-mining goals are established.

- First, you need to understand business and client objectives. You need to define what your client wants (which many times even they do not know themselves).

- Take stock of the current data mining scenario. Factor in resources, assumption, constraints, and other significant factors into your assessment.

- Using business objectives and current scenario, define your data mining goals.

- A good data mining plan is very detailed and should be developed to accomplish both business and data mining goals.

Data Understanding

In this phase, sanity check on data is performed to check whether its appropriate for the data mining goals.

- First, data is collected from multiple data sources available in the organization.

- These data sources may include multiple databases, flat filer or data cubes. There are issues like object matching and schema integration which can arise during Data Integration process. It is a quite complex and tricky process as data from various sources unlikely to match easily. For example, table A contains an entity named cust_no whereas another table B contains an entity named cust-id.

- Therefore, it is quite difficult to ensure that both of these given objects refer to the same value or not. Here, Metadata should be used to reduce errors in the data integration process.

- Next, the step is to search for properties of acquired data. A good way to explore the data is to answer the data mining questions (decided in business phase) using the query, reporting, and visualization tools.
- Based on the results of query, the data quality should be ascertained. Missing data if any should be acquired.

Data Preparation

In this phase, data is made production ready.

The data preparation process consumes about 90% of the time of the project.

The data from different sources should be selected, cleaned, transformed, formatted, anonymized, and constructed (if required).

Data cleaning is a process to "clean" the data by smoothing noisy data and filling in missing values.

For example, for a customer demographics profile, age data is missing. The data is incomplete and should be filled. In some cases, there could be data outliers. For instance, age has a value 300. Data could be inconsistent. For instance, name of the customer is different in different tables.

Data transformation operations change the data to make it useful in data mining. Following transformation can be applied.

Data Transformation

Data transformation operations would contribute toward the success of the mining process.

Smoothing: It helps to remove noise from the data.

Aggregation: Summary or aggregation operations are applied to the data. I.e., the weekly sales data is aggregated to calculate the monthly and yearly total.

Generalization: In this step, Low-level data is replaced by higher-level concepts with the help of concept hierarchies. For example, the city is replaced by the county.

Normalization: Normalization performed when the attribute data are scaled up o scaled down. Example: Data should fall in the range -2.0 to 2.0 post-normalization.

Attribute construction: These attributes are constructed and included the given set of attributes helpful for data mining.

The result of this process is a final data set that can be used in modeling.

Modelling

In this phase, mathematical models are used to determine data patterns.

- Based on the business objectives, suitable modeling techniques should be selected for the prepared dataset.

- Create a scenario to test check the quality and validity of the model.

- Run the model on the prepared dataset.

- Results should be assessed by all stakeholders to make sure that model can meet data mining objectives.

Evaluation

In this phase, patterns identified are evaluated against the business objectives.

- Results generated by the data mining model should be evaluated against the business objectives.

- Gaining business understanding is an iterative process. In fact, while understanding, new business requirements may be raised because of data mining.

- A go or no-go decision is taken to move the model in the deployment phase.

Deployment

In the deployment phase, you ship your data mining discoveries to everyday business operations.

- The knowledge or information discovered during data mining process should be made easy to understand for non-technical stakeholders.

- A detailed deployment plan, for shipping, maintenance, and monitoring of data mining discoveries is created.

- A final project report is created with lessons learned and key experiences during the project. This helps to improve the organization's business policy.

Data Mining Techniques

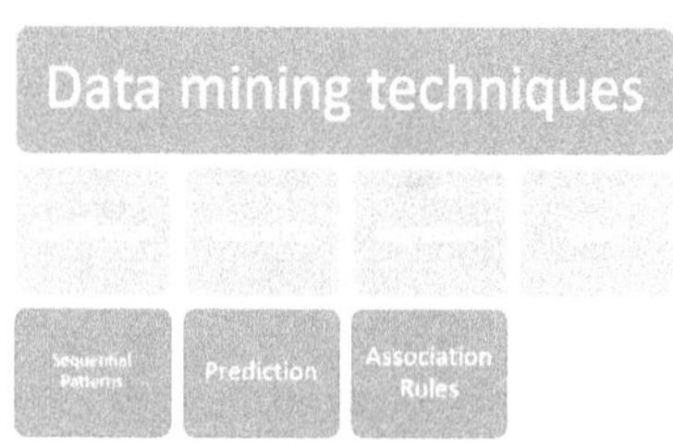

1. Classification

This analysis is used to retrieve important and relevant information about data, and metadata. This data mining method helps to classify data in different classes.

2. Clustering

Clustering analysis is a data mining technique to identify data that are like each other. This process helps to understand the differences and similarities between the data.

3. Regression

Regression analysis is the data mining method of identifying and analyzing the relationship between variables. It is used to identify the likelihood of a specific variable, given the presence of other variables.

4. Association Rules

This data mining technique helps to find the association between two or more Items. It discovers a hidden pattern in the data set.

5. Outer Detection

This type of data mining technique refers to observation of data items in the dataset which do not match an expected pattern or expected behavior. This technique can be used in a variety of domains, such as intrusion, detection, fraud or fault detection, etc. Outer detection is also called Outlier Analysis or Outlier mining.

6. Sequential Patterns

This data mining technique helps to discover or identify similar patterns or trends in transaction data for certain period.

7. Prediction

Prediction has used a combination of the other data mining techniques like trends, sequential patterns, clustering, classification, etc. It analyzes past events or instances in a right sequence for predicting a future event.

Information Retrieval

Information retrieval deals with the retrieval of information from a large number of text-based documents. Some of the database systems are not usually present in information retrieval systems because both handle different kinds of data.

Examples of information retrieval system include:

- Online Library catalogue system.
- Online Document Management Systems.
- Web Search Systems etc.

Note: The main problem in an information retrieval system is to locate relevant documents in a document collection based on a user's query. This kind of user's query consists of some keywords describing an information need.

In such search problems, the user takes an initiative to pull relevant information out from a collection. This is appropriate when the user has ad-hoc information need, i.e., a short-term need. But if the user has a long-term information need, then the retrieval system can also take an initiative to push any newly arrived information item to the user.

This kind of access to information is called Information Filtering. And the corresponding systems are known as Filtering Systems or Recommender Systems.

Basic Measures for Text Retrieval

We need to check the accuracy of a system when it retrieves a number of documents on the basis of user's input. Let the set of documents relevant to a query be denoted as {Relevant} and the set of retrieved document as {Retrieved}. The set of documents that are relevant and retrieved can be denoted as {Relevant} ∩ {Retrieved}. This can be shown in the form of a Venn diagram as follows:

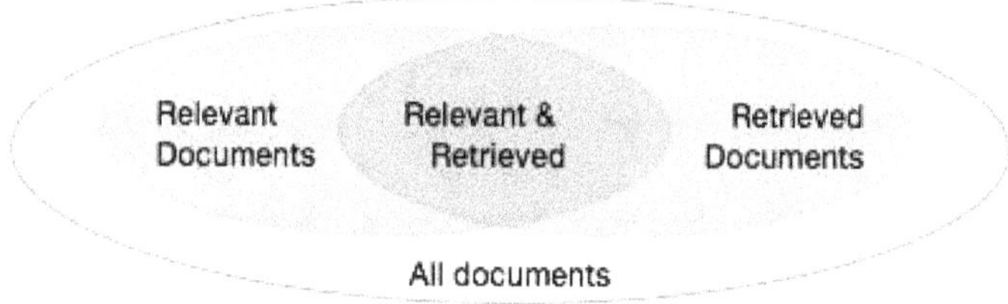

There are three fundamental measures for assessing the quality of text retrieval:

- Precision
- Recall
- F-score

Precision

Precision is the percentage of retrieved documents that are in fact relevant to the query. Precision can be defined as:

$$\text{Precision} = |\{\text{Relevant}\} \cap \{\text{Retrieved}\}| \ / \ |\{\text{Retrieved}\}|$$

Recall

Recall is the percentage of documents that are relevant to the query and were in fact retrieved. Recall is defined as:

$$\text{Recall} = |\{\text{Relevant}\} \cap \{\text{Retrieved}\}| \ / \ |\{\text{Relevant}\}|$$

F-score

F-score is the commonly used trade-off. The information retrieval system often needs to trade-off for precision or vice versa. F-score is defined as harmonic mean of recall or precision as follows.

$$\text{F-score} = \text{recall x precision} \ / \ (\text{recall} + \text{precision}) \ / \ 2$$

Challenges in Web Mining

The web poses great challenges for resource and knowledge discovery based on the following observations:

- **The web is too huge:** The size of the web is very huge and rapidly increasing. This seems that the web is too huge for data warehousing and data mining.

- **Complexity of Web pages:** The web pages do not have unifying structure. They are very complex as compared to traditional text document. There are huge amount of documents in digital library of web. These libraries are not arranged according to any particular sorted order.

- **Web is dynamic information source:** The information on the web is rapidly updated. The data such as news, stock markets, weather, sports, shopping, etc., are regularly updated.

- **Diversity of user communities:** The user community on the web is rapidly expanding. These users have different backgrounds, interests, and usage purposes. There are more than 100 million workstations that are connected to the Internet and still rapidly increasing.

- **Relevancy of Information:** It is considered that a particular person is generally interested in only small portion of the web, while the rest of the portion of the web contains the information that is not relevant to the user and may swamp desired results.

1.12. Specialty Databases

Database Users and Administrators

There will be different types of users depending on their need and way of accessing the database.

- **Application Programmers:** They are the developers who interact with the database by means of DML queries. These DML queries are written in the application programs like C, C++, JAVA, Pascal etc. These queries are converted into object code to communicate with the database.

- **Sophisticated Users:** They are database developers, who write SQL queries to select/insert/delete/update data. They do not use any application or programs to request the database. They directly interact with the database by means of query language like SQL.

- **Specialized Users:** These are also sophisticated users, but they write special database application programs. They are the developers who develop the complex programs to the requirement.

- **Stand-alone Users:** These users will have stand–alone database for their personal use. These kinds of database will have readymade database packages which will have menus and graphical interfaces.

- **Native Users:** These are the users who use the existing application to interact with the database. For example, online library system, ticket booking systems, ATMs etc which has existing application and users use them to interact with the database to fulfill their requests.

There will be unused memory in database, making the memory inevitably huge. These administration and maintenance of database is taken care by database Administrator – DBA. A DBA has many responsibilities. A good performing database is in the hands of DBA.

- **Installing and upgrading the DBMS Servers:** DBA is responsible for installing a new DBMS server for the new projects. He is also responsible for upgrading these servers as there are new versions comes in the market or requirement. If there is any failure in upgradation of the existing servers, he should be able revert the new changes back to the older version, thus maintaining the DBMS working. He is also responsible for updating the service packs/ hot fixes/ patches to the DBMS servers.

- **Design and implementation:** Designing the database and implementing is also DBA's responsibility. He should be able to decide proper memory management, file organizations, error handling, log maintenance etc for the database.

- **Performance tuning:** Since database is huge and it will have lots of tables, data, constraints and indices, there will be variations in the performance from time to time. Also, because of some designing issues or data growth, the database will not work as expected. It is responsibility of the DBA to tune the database performance. He is responsible to make sure all the queries and programs works in fraction of seconds.

- **Migrate database servers:** Sometimes, users using oracle would like to shift to SQL server or Netezza. It is the responsibility of DBA to make sure that migration happens without any failure, and there is no data loss.

- **Backup and Recovery:** Proper backup and recovery programs needs to be developed by DBA and has to be maintained him. This is one of the main responsibilities of DBA. Data/objects should be backed up regularly so that if there is any crash, it should be recovered without much effort and data loss.

- **Security:** DBA is responsible for creating various database users and roles, and giving them different levels of access rights.

- **Documentation:** DBA should be properly documenting all his activities so that if he quits or any new DBA comes in, he should be able to understand the database without any effort. He should basically maintain all his installation, backup, recovery, security methods. He should keep various reports about database performance.

History of Database Systems

- 1950s and early 1960s:
  - Data processing using magnetic tapes for storage.
- Tapes provide only sequential access.
  - Punched cards for input.

- Late 1960s and 1970s:
  - Hard disks allow direct access to data.
  - Network and hierarchical data models in widespread use.
  - Ted Codd defines the relational data model.
- Would win the ACM Turing Award for this work.
- IBM Research begins System R prototype.
- UC Berkeley begins Ingres prototype.
  - High-performance (for the era) transaction processing.
- 1980s:
  - Research relational prototypes evolve into commercial systems.
- SQL becomes industry standard.
  - Parallel and distributed database systems.
  - Object-oriented database systems.
- 1990s:
  - Large decision support and data-mining applications.
  - Large multi-tera byte data warehouses.
  - Emergence of Web commerce.
- 2000s:
  - XML and XQuery standards.
  - Automated database administration.
  - Increasing use of highly parallel database systems.
  - Web-scale distributed data storage systems.

1.13. Introduction to Data base Design

Database Design and ER Diagrams

Let us create a simple ER diagram for a STUDENT database. What is the requirement of this database?

'Student attends class. Each class is divided into one or more sections. Each class will have its own specified subjects. Students have to attend all the subjects of the class that he attends'.

Now let us identify what are the entities? STUDENT, CLASS, SECTION, SUBJECT are the entities. Attributes of these entities are not specified here. But we know what could be the entities of each of the entities. We can list them as below at this point of time.

STUDENT	CLASS	SECTION	SUBJECT
STUDENT_ID	CLASS_ID	SECTION_ID	SUBJECT_ID
STUDENT_NAME	CLASS_NAME	SECTION_NAME	SUBJECT_NAME
ADDRESS			
DOB			
AGE			
CLASS_ID			
SECTION_ID			

What are the relationships we have? 'Attends', 'has section', 'have subjects' and 'studies subjects' are the relations here. With this knowledge of requirement, we can draw the ER diagram as below.

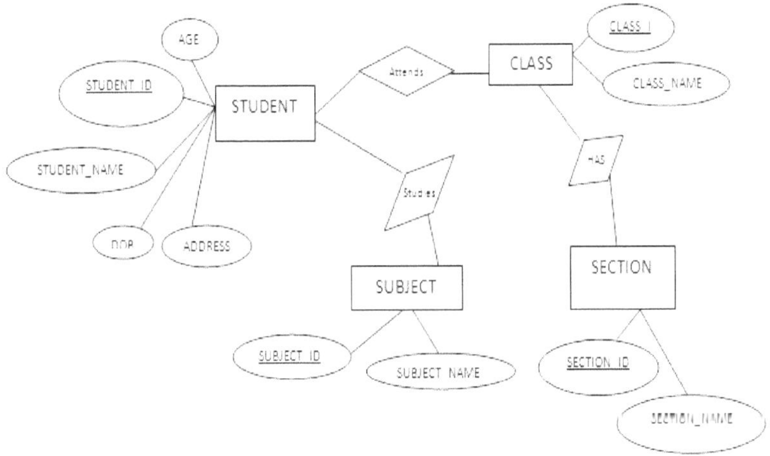

Observe the diagram carefully. Did we miss or drew it correctly? Are we missing anything on the diagram? Is it inferring correct requirement? What are our observations?

- Age attribute can be derived from DOB. Hence we have to draw dashed oval.

- Address is a composite attribute. We have to draw its sub attributes too. So that we will be very clear about his address details.

- If we see the SECTION entity, by section id, will we be able get the section that student attends? There is no relation mentioned between Student and Section. But Section is mapped only with Class. What do we understand from this? Section is a weak entity. Hence we have to represent it properly.

- If we look at 'attends' relationship between STUDENT and CLASS, we can have 'Joining Date' and 'Total Number of Hours' attributes. But it is an attribute of relation. We have to show them in the diagram.

- Since each class is having different subjects and Students attends those subjects, we can modify the relation 'studies' to 'has' relation on the **relation** 'attends'.

Now the diagram will change to reflect all above points.

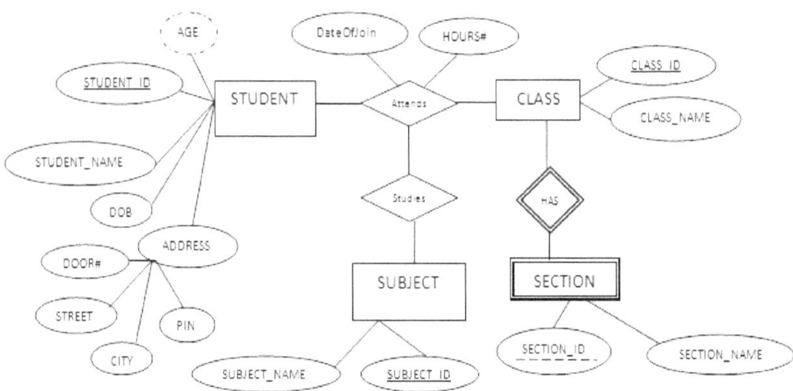

Are done with complete diagram? We have not added the cardinality and participation in the diagram.

What are the Participation Constraints Here?

- All the Students attend any one of the class, but class can have only certain group of students. Hence total participation of Students and partial participation of class in 'Attends' relation.

- All the class has section and all the section has class. Hence both are total participation.

- All the Students study some of the subjects specific for their class and each class has only some group of subjects. Hence partial participation of both STUDENT and CLASS. Each subject will be studied by some students and it will be part of some class. Hence this also partial participation.

What are the Cardinalities of All the Relationship?

- Each Student attends only one class at a time. Hence it is a **1: 1** relation.

- Each class has one or more sections. Hence it can be considered as **1: N** relation.

- Each student attends many subjects and each class has many subjects. Hence it is a **1: N** relation.

Note: If you look at STUDENT and CLASS relationship as many Students attend one class, then it would be an **M: 1** relation. It is all up to the developer, how he looks at the requirement.

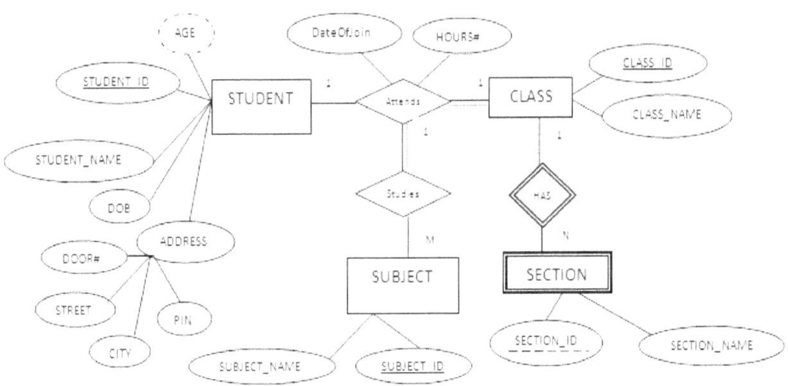

Now it is a complete ER diagram for simple Student database.

Additional Features of ER Model

- Generalization

- Specialization

- Aggregation

Generalization is a bottom-up approach in which two lower level entities combine to form a higher level entity. In generalization, the higher level entity can also combine with other lower level entities to make further higher level entity.

It's more like Super class and Subclass system, but the only difference is the approach, which is bottom-up. Hence, entities are combined to form a more generalized entity, in other words, sub-classes are combined to form a super-class.

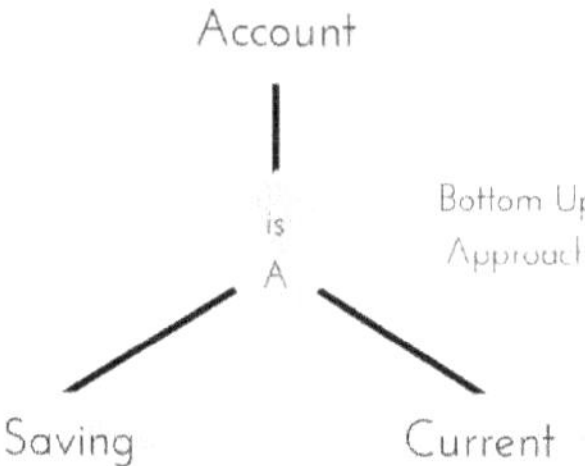

For example, **Saving** and **Current** account types entities can be generalized and an entity with name **Account** can be created, which covers both.

Specialization is opposite to Generalization. It is a top-down approach in which one higher level entity can be broken down into two lower level entity. In specialization, a higher level entity may not have any lower-level entity sets, it's possible.

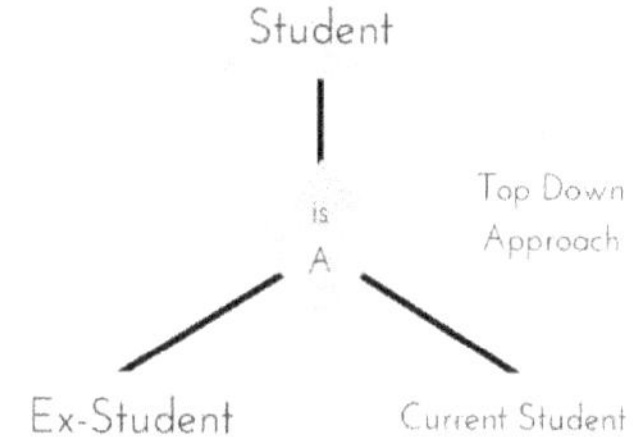

Aggregation is a process when relation between two entities is treated as a **single entity**.

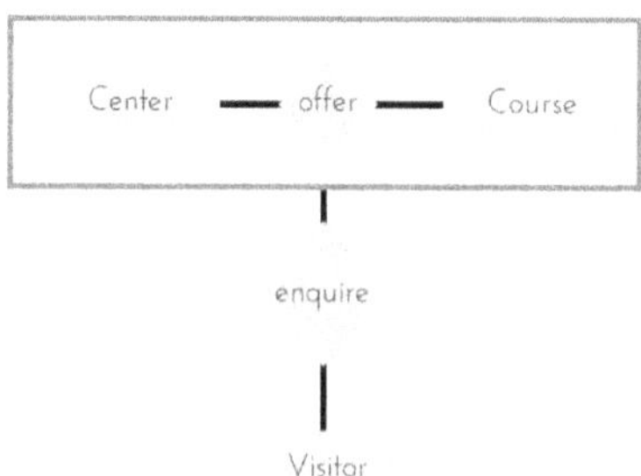

Conceptual Design with the ER Model

- Design choices:
    - Should a concept be modeled as an entity or an attribute?
    - Should a concept be modeled as an entity or a relationship?
    - Identifying relationships: Binary or ternary? Aggregation?
- Constraints in the ER Model:
    - A lot of data semantics can (and should) be captured.
    - But some constraints cannot be captured in ER diagrams.

Entity vs. Attribute

- Should *address* be an attribute of Employees or an entity (connected to Employees by a relationship)?
- Depends upon the use we want to make of address information, and the semantics of the data:
    - If we have several addresses per employee, *address* must be an entity.
    - (Since attributes cannot be set-valued).
- If the structure (city, street, etc.) is important, e.g., we want to retrieve employees in a given city, *address* must be modeled as an entity (since attribute values are atomic).

Conceptual Design for Large Enterprises

- Conceptual design follows requirements analysis.
    - Yields a high-level description of data to be stored.
- ER model popular for conceptual design.
    - Constructs are expressive, close to the way people think about their applications.
- Basic constructs: *entities*, *relationships*, and *attributes* (of entities and relationships).
- Some additional constructs: weak entities, ISA hierarchies, and aggregation.
- Note: There are many variations on ER model.
- Several kinds of integrity constraints can be expressed in the ER model: *key constraints*, *participation constraints*, and *overlap/covering constraints* for ISA hierarchies. Some *foreign key constraints* are also implicit in the definition of a relationship set.
    - Some constraints (notably, *functional dependencies*) cannot be expressed in the ER model.

- Constraints play an important role in determining the best database design for an enterprise.
- ER design is *subjective*. There are often many ways to model a given scenario! Analyzing alternatives can be tricky, especially for a large enterprise. Common choices include:
  - Entity vs. attribute, entity vs. relationship, binary or n-ary relationship, whether or not to use ISA hierarchies, and whether or not to use aggregation.

Ensuring good database design: resulting relational schema should be analyzed and refined further. FD information and normalization techniques are especially useful.

Introduction to the Relational Model

Relational model can represent as a table with columns and rows. Each row is known as a tuple. Each table of the column has a name or attribute.

- **Domain:** It contains a set of atomic values that an attribute can take.
- **Attribute:** It contains the name of a column in a particular table. Each attribute Ai must have a domain, dom(Ai).
- **Relational instance:** In the relational database system, the relational instance is represented by a finite set of tuples. Relation instances do not have duplicate tuples.
- **Relational schema:** A relational schema contains the name of the relation and name of all columns or attributes.
- **Relational key:** In the relational key, each row has one or more attributes. It can identify the row in the relation uniquely.

Example: STUDENT Relation

NAME	ROLL_NO	PHONE_NO	ADDRESS	AGE
Ram	14795	7305758992	Noida	24
Shyam	12839	9026288936	Delhi	35
Laxman	33289	8583287182	Gurugram	20
Mahesh	27857	7086819134	Ghaziabad	27
Ganesh	17282	9028 9i3988	Delhi	40

- In the given table, NAME, ROLL_NO, PHONE_NO, ADDRESS, and AGE are the attributes.
- The instance of schema STUDENT has 5 tuples.
- t3 = <Laxman, 33289, 8583287182, Gurugram, 20>.

Properties of Relations

- Name of the relation is distinct from all other relations.
- Each relation cell contains exactly one atomic (single) value.
- Each attribute contains a distinct name.
- Attribute domain has no significance.
- tuple has no duplicate value.
- Order of tuple can have a different sequence.

Relational Algebra

Relational algebra is a procedural query language. It gives a step by step process to obtain the result of the query. It uses operators to perform queries.

Types of Relational Operation

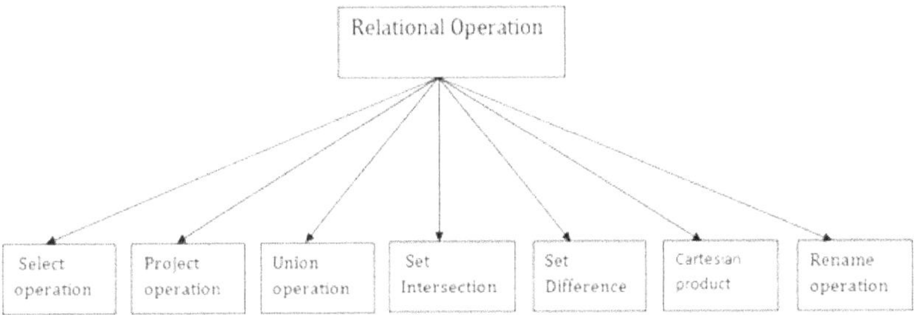

1. Select Operation

- The select operation selects tuples that satisfy a given predicate.
- It is denoted by sigma (σ).

Notation: $\sigma\ p(r)$

Where:

σ is used for selection prediction is used for relation p is used as a propositional logic formula which may use connectors like: AND OR and NOT.

These relational can use as relational operators like $=, \neq, \geq, <, >, \leq$.

For example: LOAN Relation

BRANCH_NAME	LOAN_NO	AMOUNT
Downtown	L-17	1000
Redwood	L-23	2000
Perryride	L-15	1500
Downtown	L-14	1500
Mianus	L-13	500
Roundhill	L-11	900
Perryride	L-16	1300

Input:

σ BRANCH_NAME="perryride" (LOAN)

Output:

BRANCH_NAME	LOAN_NO	AMOUNT
Perryride	L-15	1500
Perryride	L-16	1300

2. Project Operation

- This operation shows the list of those attributes that we wish to appear in the result. Rest of the attributes are eliminated from the table.

- It is denoted by $\prod$.

   Notation: $\prod$ A1, A2, An (r)

Where

A1, A2, A3 is used as an attribute name of relation r.

Example: CUSTOMER RELATION

NAME	STREET	CITY
Jones	Main	Harrison
Smith	North	Rye
Hays	Main	Harrison
Curry	North	Rye
Johnson	Alma	Brooklyn
Brooks	Senator	Brooklyn

Input:

∏ NAME, CITY (CUSTOMER)

Output:

NAME	CITY
Jones	Harrison
Smith	Rye
Hays	Harrison
Curry	Rye
Johnson	Brooklyn
Brooks	Brooklyn

3. Union Operation

- Suppose there are two tuples R and S. The union operation contains all the tuples that are either in R or S or both in R & S.

- It eliminates the duplicate tuples. It is denoted by ∪.

*Notation: R * S*

A union operation must hold the following condition:

- R and S must have the attribute of the same number.

- Duplicate tuples are eliminated automatically.

Example:

DEPOSITOR RELATION

CUSTOMER_NAME	ACCOUNT_NO
Johnson	A-101
Smith	A-121
Mayes	A-321
Turner	A-176
Johnson	A-273
Jones	A-472
Lindsay	A-284

BORROW RELATION

CUSTOMER_NAME	LOAN_NO
Jones	L-17
Smith	L-23
Hayes	L-15
Jackson	L-14
Curry	L-93
Smith	L-11
Williams	L-17

Input:

∏ CUSTOMER_NAME (BORROW) ∪ ∏ CUSTOMER_NAME (DEPOSITOR)

Output:

CUSTOMER_NAME
Johnson
Smith
Hayes
Turner
Jones
Lindsay
Jackson
Curry
Williams
Mayes

4. Set Intersection

- Suppose there are two tuples R and S. The set intersection operation contains all tuples that are in both R & S.
- It is denoted by intersection ∩.

Notation: R ∩ S

Example: Using the above DEPOSITOR table and BORROW table.

Input

∏ CUSTOMER_NAME (BORROW) ∩ ∏ CUSTOMER_NAME (DEPOSITOR)

Output

CUSTOMER_NAME
Smith
Jones

5. Set Difference

- Suppose there are two tuples R and S. The set intersection operation contains all tuples that are in R but not in S.
- It is denoted by intersection minus (-).

  Notation: R - S

  Example: Using the above DEPOSITOR table and BORROW table.

Input

∏ CUSTOMER_NAME (BORROW) - ∏ CUSTOMER_NAME (DEPOSITOR)

Output

CUSTOMER_NAME
Jackson
Hayes
Willians
Curry

6. Cartesian Product

- The Cartesian product is used to combine each row in one table with each row in the other table. It is also known as a cross product.
- It is denoted by X.

  Notation: E X D

Example

EMPLOYEE

EMP_ID	EMP_NAME	EMP_DEPT
1	Smith	A
2	Harry	C
3	John	B

DEPARTMENT

DEPT_NO	DEPT_NAME
A	Marketing
B	Sales
C	Legal

Input

EMPLOYEE X DEPARTMENT

Output

EMP_ID	EMP_NAME	EMP_DEPT	DEPT_NO	DEPT_NAME
1	Smith	A	A	Marketing
1	Smith	A	B	Sales
1	Smith	A	C	Legal
2	Harry	C	A	Marketing
2	Harry	C	B	Sales
2	Harry	C	C	Legal
3	John	B	A	Marketing
3	John	B	B	Sales
3	John	B	C	Legal

7. Rename Operation

The rename operation is used to rename the output relation. It is denoted by rho (ρ).

Example: We can use the rename operator to rename STUDENT relation to STUDENT1.

ρ(STUDENT1, STUDENT).

Join Operations

A Join operation combines related tuples from different relations, if and only if a given join condition is satisfied. It is denoted by ⋈.

Example

EMP_CODE	EMP_NAME
101	Stephan
102	Jack
103	Harry

SALARY

EMP_CODE	SALARY
101	50000
102	30000
103	25000

Operation: (EMPLOYEE ⋈ SALARY).

Result

EMP_CODE	EMP_NAME	SALARY
101	Stephan	50000
102	Jack	30000
103	Harry	25000

Types of Join Operations

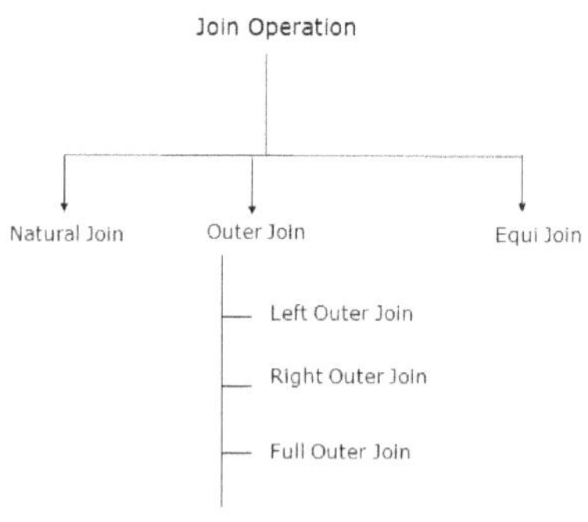

1. Natural Join

- A natural join is the set of tuples of all combinations in R and S that are equal on their common attribute names.

- It is denoted by ⋈.

Example: Let's use the above EMPLOYEE table and SALARY table:

Input

∏EMP_NAME, SALARY (EMPLOYEE ⋈ SALARY)

Output

EMP_NAME	SALARY
Stephan	50000
Jack	30000
Harry	25000

2. Outer Join

The outer join operation is an extension of the join operation. It is used to deal with missing information.

Example:

Employee

EMP_NAME	STREET	CITY
Ram	Civil line	Mumbai
Shyam	Park street	Kolkata
Ravi	M.G. Street	Delhi
Hari	Nehru nagar	Hyderabad

Fact_Workers

EMP_NAME	BRANCH	SALARY
Ram	Infosys	10000
Shyam	Wipro	20000
Kuber	HCL	30000
Hari	TCS	50000

Input:

(EMPLOYEE ⋈ FACT_WORKERS)

Output:

EMP_NAME	STREET	CITY	BRANCH	SALARY
Ram	Civil line	Mumbai	Infosys	10000
Shyam	Park street	Kolkata	Wipro	20000
Hari	Nehru nagar	Hyderabad	TCS	50000

An outer join is basically of three types:

- Left outer join
- Right outer join
- Full outer join

a. Left Outer Join

- Left outer join contains the set of tuples of all combinations in R and S that are equal on their common attribute names.
- In the left outer join, tuples in R have no matching tuples in S.
- It is denoted by ⋈.

Example: Using the above EMPLOYEE table and FACT_WORKERS table.

Input

EMPLOYEE ⋈ FACT_WORKERS

EMP_NAME	STREET	CITY	BRANCH	SALARY
Ram	Civil line	Mumbai	Infosys	10000
Shyam	Park street	Kolkata	Wipro	20000
Hari	Nehru street	Hyderabad	TCS	50000
Ravi	M.G. Street	Delhi	NULL	NULL

b. Right Outer Join

- Right outer join contains the set of tuples of all combinations in R and S that are equal on their common attribute names.
- In right outer join, tuples in S have no matching tuples in R.
- It is denoted by ⋈.

Example: Using the above EMPLOYEE table and FACT_WORKERS Relation.

Input

EMPLOYEE ⋈ FACT_WORKERS

Output

EMP_NAME	BRANCH	SALARY	STREET	CITY
Ram	Infosys	10000	Civil line	Mumbai
Shyam	Wipro	20000	Park street	Kolkata
Hari	TCS	50000	Nehru street	Hyderabad
Kuber	HCL	30000	NULL	NULL

c. Full Outer Join

- Full outer join is like a left or right join except that it contains all rows from both tables.
- In full outer join, tuples in R that have no matching tuples in S and tuples in S that have no matching tuples in R in their common attribute name.
- It is denoted by ⋈.

Example: Using the above EMPLOYEE table and FACT_WORKERS table.

Input

EMPLOYEE ⋈ FACT_WORKERS

Output

EMP_NAME	STREET	CITY	BRANCH	SALARY
Ram	Civil line	Mumbai	Infosys	10000
Shyam	Park street	Kolkata	Wipro	20000
Hari	Nehru street	Hyderabad	TCS	50000
Ravi	M.G. Street	Delhi	NULL	NULL
Kuber	NULL	NULL	HCL	30000

3. Equi Join

It is also known as an inner join. It is the most common join. It is based on matched data as per the equality condition. The equi join uses the comparison operator (=).

Example

CLASS_ID	NAME
1	John
2	Harry
3	Jackson

Product

PRODUCT_ID	CITY
1	Delhi
2	Mumbai
3	Noida

Input:

CUSTOMER ⋈ PRODUCT

Output:

CLASS_ID	NAME	PRODUCT_ID	CITY
1	John	1	Delhi
2	Harry	2	Mumbai
3	Harry	3	Noida

Integrity Constraints over Relations

- Integrity constraints are a set of rules. It is used to maintain the quality of information.

- Integrity constraints ensure that the data insertion, updating, and other processes have to be performed in such a way that data integrity is not affected.

- Thus, integrity constraint is used to guard against accidental damage to the database.

Types of Integrity Constraint

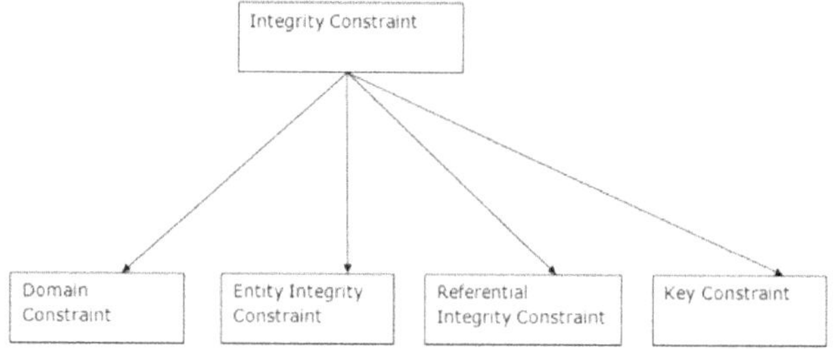

1. Domain Constraints

- Domain constraints can be defined as the definition of a valid set of values for an attribute.

- The data type of domain includes string, character, integer, time, date, currency, etc. The value of the attribute must be available in the corresponding domain.

Example:

ID	NAME	SEMENSTER	AGE
1000	Tom	1st	17
1001	Johnson	2nd	24
1002	Leonardo	5th	21
1003	Kate	3rd	19
1004	Morgan	8th	A

Not allowed. Because AGE is an integer attribute

2. Entity Integrity Constraints

- The entity integrity constraint states that primary key value can't be null.

- This is because the primary key value is used to identify individual rows in relation and if the primary key has a null value, then we can't identify those rows.

- A table can contain a null value other than the primary key field.

Example

EMPLOYEE

EMP_ID	EMP_NAME	SALARY
123	Jack	30000
142	Harry	60000
164	John	20000
	Jackson	27000

Not allowed as primary key can't contain a NULL value

3. Referential Integrity Constraints

- A referential integrity constraint is specified between two tables.

- In the Referential integrity constraints, if a foreign key in Table 1 refers to the Primary Key of Table 2, then every value of the Foreign Key in Table 1 must be null or be available in Table 2.

Example

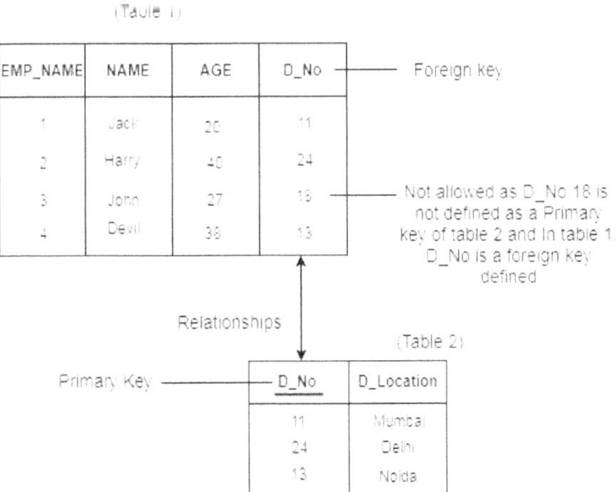

4. Key Constraints

- Keys are the entity set that is used to identify an entity within its entity set uniquely.

- An entity set can have multiple keys, but out of which one key will be the primary key. A primary key can contain a unique and null value in the relational table.

Example

ID	NAME	SEMENSTER	AGE
1000	Tom	1st	17
1001	Johnson	2nd	24
1002	Leonardo	5th	21
1003	Kate	3rd	19
1002	Morgan	8th	22

Not allowed. Because all row must be unique

Enforcing Integrity Constraints

Constraints are the rules enforced on the data columns of a table. These are used to limit the type of data that can go into a table. This ensures the accuracy and reliability of the data in the database.

Constraints could be either on a column level or a table level. The column level constraints are applied only to one column, whereas the table level constraints are applied to the whole table.

Following are some of the most commonly used constraints available in SQL. These constraints have already been discussed in SQL - RDBMS Concepts chapter, but it's worth to revise them at this point.

- **NOT NULL Constraint:** Ensures that a column cannot have NULL value.

- **DEFAULT Constraint:** Provides a default value for a column when none is specified.

- **UNIQUE Constraint:** Ensures that all values in a column are different.

- **PRIMARY Key:** Uniquely identifies each row/record in a database table.

- **FOREIGN Key:** Uniquely identifies a row/record in any of the given database table.

- **CHECK Constraint:** The CHECK constraint ensures that all the values in a column satisfies certain conditions.

- **INDEX:** Used to create and retrieve data from the database very quickly.

Constraints can be specified when a table is created with the CREATE TABLE statement or you can use the ALTER TABLE statement to create constraints even after the table is created.

Dropping Constraints

Any constraint that you have defined can be dropped using the ALTER TABLE command with the DROP CONSTRAINT option.

For example, to drop the primary key constraint in the EMPLOYEES table, you can use the following command.

ALTER TABLE EMPLOYEES DROP CONSTRAINT EMPLOYEES_PK;

Some implementations may provide shortcuts for dropping certain constraints. For example, to drop the primary key constraint for a table in Oracle, you can use the following command.

ALTER TABLE EMPLOYEES DROP PRIMARY KEY;

Querying Relational Data, Logical Data Base Design

ER Model, when conceptualized into diagrams, gives a good overview of entity-relationship, which is easier to understand. ER diagrams can be mapped to relational schema, that is, it is possible to create relational schema using ER diagram. We cannot import all the ER constraints into relational model, but an approximate schema can be generated.

There are several processes and algorithms available to convert ER Diagrams into Relational Schema. Some of them are automated and some of them are manual. We may focus here on the mapping diagram contents to relational basics.

ER diagrams mainly comprise of:

- Entity and its attributes.
- Relationship, which is association among entities.

Mapping Entity

An entity is a real-world object with some attributes.

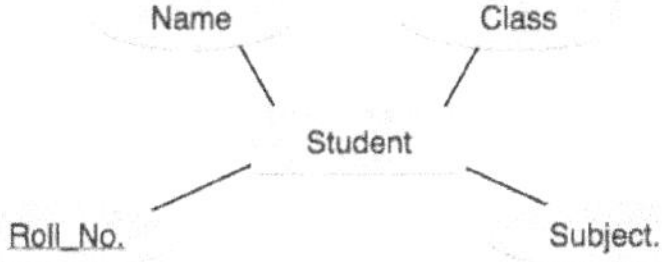

Mapping Process (Algorithm)

- Create table for each entity.
- Entity's attributes should become fields of tables with their respective data types.
- Declare primary key.

Mapping Relationship

A relationship is an association among entities.

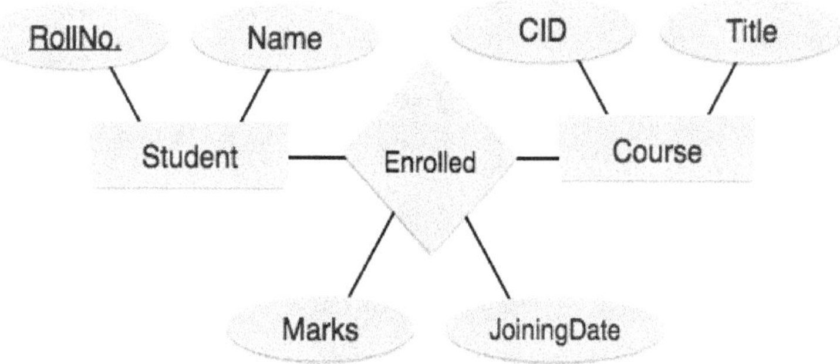

Mapping Process

- Create table for a relationship.
- Add the primary keys of all participating Entities as fields of table with their respective data types.
- If relationship has any attribute, add each attribute as field of table.
- Declare a primary key composing all the primary keys of participating entities.
- Declare all foreign key constraints.

Mapping Weak Entity Sets

A weak entity set is one which does not have any primary key associated with it.

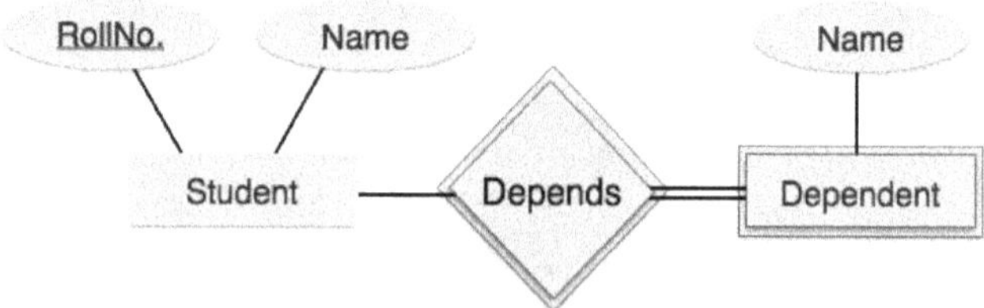

Mapping Process

- Create table for weak entity set.
- Add all its attributes to table as field.
- Add the primary key of identifying entity set.
- Declare all foreign key constraints.

Mapping Hierarchical Entities

ER specialization or generalization comes in the form of hierarchical entity sets.

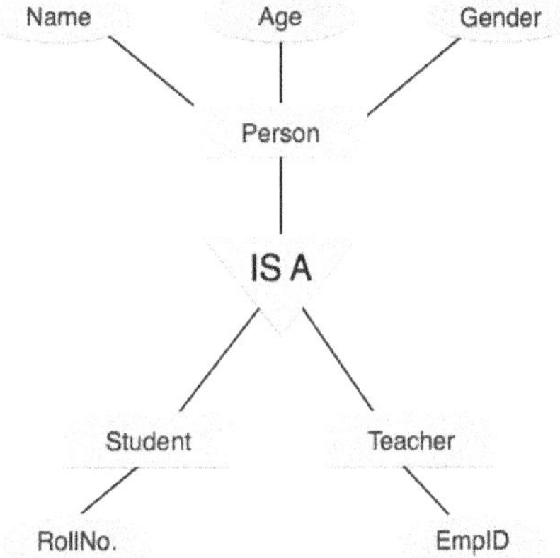

Mapping Process

- Create tables for all higher-level entities.
- Create tables for lower-level entities.
- Add primary keys of higher-level entities in the table of lower-level entities.
- In lower-level tables, add all other attributes of lower-level entities.
- Declare primary key of higher-level table and the primary key for lower-level table.
- Declare foreign key constraints.

Introduction to Views, Destroying / Altering Tables and Views

- Virtual tables

CREATE VIEW YoungActiveStudents (name,grade) AS SELECT S.name, E.grade FROM Students S, Enrolled E WHERE S.sid=E.sid and S.age

Views and Security

- DBA: grants authorization to a view for a user.
- user can only see the view - nothing else.

Table Changes

- DROP TABLE
- ALTER TABLE

e.g.

ALTER TABLE students.

ADD COLUMN maiden-name CHAR(10).

2. Relational Algebra and Calculus

2.1.   Introduction

Relational algebra is a procedural query language, which takes instances of relations as input and yields instances of relations as output. It uses operators to perform queries. An operator can be either **unary** or **binary**.

The fundamental operations of relational algebra are as follows:

- Select
- Project
- Union
- Set different
- Cartesian product
- Rename

Select Operation (σ)

It selects tuples that satisfy the given predicate from a relation.

Notation: $\sigma_p(r)$

Where **σ** stands for selection predicate and **r** stands for relation. *p* is prepositional logic formula which may use connectors like **and**, **or**, and **not**. These terms may use relational operators like – =, ≠, ≥, <, >, ≤.

For Example

$$\sigma_{subject = \text{"database"}}(Books)$$

Output: Selects tuples from books where subject is 'database'.

$$\sigma_{subject = \text{"database" and price = "450"}}(Books)$$

Output: Selects tuples from books where subject is 'database' and 'price' is 450.

$$\sigma_{subject = \text{"database" and price = "450" or year > "2010"}}(Books)$$

Output: Selects tuples from books where subject is 'database' and 'price' is 450 or those books published after 2010.

Project Operation (∏)

It projects column(s) that satisfy a given predicate.

Notation: $\prod_{A_1, A_2, An} (r)$

Where A_1, A_2, A_n are attribute names of relation **r**.

Duplicate rows are automatically eliminated, as relation is a set.

For Example

$$\prod_{subject, author} (Books)$$

Selects and projects columns named as subject and author from the relation Books.

Union Operation (∪)

It performs binary union between two given relations and is defined as,

$$r \cup s = \{t \mid t \in r \text{ or } t \in s\}$$

Notation: r U s

Where **r** and **s** are either database relations or relation result set (temporary relation).

For a union operation to be valid, the following conditions must hold.

- **r**, and **s** must have the same number of attributes.
- Attribute domains must be compatible.
- Duplicate tuples are automatically eliminated.

$$\prod_{author} (Books) \cup \prod_{author} (Articles)$$

Output: Projects the names of the authors who have either written a book or an article or both.

Set Difference (−)

The result of set difference operation is tuples, which are present in one relation but are not in the second relation.

Notation: r − s

Finds all the tuples that are present in **r** but not in **s**.

$$\prod_{author} (Books) - \prod_{author} (Articles)$$

Output: Provides the name of authors who have written books but not articles.

Cartesian Product (X)

Combines information of two different relations into one.

Notation: r X s

Where **r** and **s** are relations and their output will be defined as,

$$r \text{ X } s = \{q\ t \mid q \in r \text{ and } t \in s\}$$

$$\sigma_{\text{author = 'tutorialspoint'}}(\text{Books X Articles})$$

Output: Yields a relation, which shows all the books and articles written by tutorials point.

Rename Operation (ρ)

The results of relational algebra are also relations but without any name. The rename operation allows us to rename the output relation. 'rename' operation is denoted with small Greek letter **rho** ρ.

Notation: ρ_x (E)

Where the result of expression **E** is saved with name of **x**.

Additional operations are:

- Set intersection
- Assignment
- Natural join

2.2.   Relational Calculus

In contrast to Relational Algebra, Relational Calculus is a non-procedural query language, that is, it tells what to do but never explains how to do it.

Relational calculus exists in two forms.

- Tuple Relational Calculus (TRC).
- Filtering variable ranges over tuples.

Notation: {T | Condition}

Returns all tuples T that satisfies a condition.

For Example

$$\{T.name \mid Author(T) \text{ AND } T.article = \text{'database'}\}$$

Output: Returns tuples with 'name' from Author who has written article on 'database'.

TRC can be quantified. We can use Existential ($\exists$) and Universal Quantifiers ($\forall$).

For Example

$$\{R| \; \exists T \in Authors(T.article='database' \; AND \; R.name=T.name)\}$$

Output: The above query will yield the same result as the previous one.

Domain Relational Calculus (DRC)

In DRC, the filtering variable uses the domain of attributes instead of entire tuple values (as done in TRC, mentioned above).

Notation

$$\{a_1, a_2, a_3,..., a_n \; | \; P \; (a_1, a_2, a_3,...,a_n)\}$$

Where a1, a2 are attributes and **P** stands for formulae built by inner attributes.

For Example

$$\{< article, page, subject > \; | \; \in TutorialsPoint \land subject = 'database'\}$$

Output: Yields Article, Page, and Subject from the relation TutorialsPoint, where subject is database.

2.3.   Expressive Power of Algebra and Calculus

Just like TRC, DRC can also be written using existential and universal quantifiers. DRC also involves relational operators.

The expression power of Tuple Relation Calculus and Domain Relation Calculus is equivalent to Relational Algebra.

Unsafe query z a syntactically correct calculus query that has an infinite number of answers z E.g., $\{S \; | \; \neg \; (S \in Sailors)\}$.

Every query that can be expressed in relational algebra can be expressed as a safe query in DRC / TRC; the converse is also true.

Relational Completeness z Query language (e.g., SQL) can express every query that is expressible in relational algebra.

In addition, commercial query languages can express some queries that cannot be expressed in relational algebra.

2.4.   SQL

SQL is Structured Query Language, which is a computer language for storing, manipulating and retrieving data stored in a relational database.

SQL is the standard language for Relational Database System. All the Relational Database Management Systems (RDMS) like MySQL, MS Access, Oracle, Sybase, Informix, Postgres and SQL Server use SQL as their standard database language.

Advantage of SQL

- It is a high level language that provides greater degree of abstraction.
- Increased acceptance and availability of SQL.
- Simple and easy to learn.
- SQL can handle complex situations.

SQL Data Types

- CHAR(n)-fixed length string of exactly 'n' character.
- VARCHAR(n)- varying length string.
- FLOAT- floating point number.

SQL Operators

Arithmetic operators-> (/, *, -, +)

Comparison operators-> (=,>,<,<=,>=,IN,ANY,ALL,SOME,BETWEEN,EXISTS)   Logical operators-> (AND, OR, NOT)

Set operators-> (UNION,UNIONALL,INTERSECT,MINUS)

All the SQL statements start with any of the keywords like SELECT, INSERT, UPDATE, DELETE, ALTER, DROP, CREATE, USE, SHOW and the entire statements end with a semicolon (;).

Types of SQL Commands

SQL statements are divided into following types:

- **Data Definition Language (DDL) -** Used to create, alter and] delete database.
- **Data Manipulation Language (DML) -** Used to insert, modify and delete the data.
- **Data Query Language (DQL) -** Enables the users to query one or more tables to get the information they want.
- **Data Control Language (DCL) -** Controls the user access to the database.
- **Transaction Control Statements (TCS)** - Manage all the changes made by the DML statements.

SQL SELECT Statement
SELECT column1, column2....columnN
FROM table_name;

SQL DISTINCT Clause
SELECT DISTINCT column1, column2....columnN
FROM table_name;

SQL WHERE Clause
SELECT column1, column2....columnN
FROM table_name
WHERE CONDITION;

SQL AND/OR Clause
SELECT column1, column2....columnN
FROM table_name
WHERE CONDITION-1 {AND|OR} CONDITION-2;

SQL IN Clause
SELECT column1, column2....columnN
FROM table_name
WHERE column_name IN (val-1, val-2,...val-N);

SQL BETWEEN Clause
SELECT column1, column2....columnN
FROM table_name
WHERE column_name BETWEEN val-1 AND val-2;

SQL LIKE Clause
SELECT column1, column2....columnN
FROM table_name
WHERE column_name LIKE {PATTERN};

SQL ORDER BY Clause
SELECT column1, column2....columnN
FROM table_name
WHERE CONDITION
ORDER BY column_name {ASC|DESC};

SQL GROUP BY Clause
SELECT SUM (column_name)

FROM table_name

WHERE CONDITION

GROUP BY column_name;

SQL COUNT Clause
SELECT COUNT (column_name)

FROM table_name

WHERE CONDITION;

SQL HAVING Clause
SELECT SUM(column_name)

FROM table_name

WHERE CONDITION

GROUP BY column_name

HAVING (arithmetic function condition);

SQL CREATE TABLE Statement
CREATE TABLE table_name (

column1 datatype,

column2 datatype,

column3 datatype,

.....

ColumnN datatype,

PRIMARY KEY (one or more columns)

);

SQL DROP TABLE Statement
DROP TABLE table_name;

SQL CREATE INDEX Statement
CREATE UNIQUE INDEX index_name

ON table_name (column1, column2,...columnN);

SQL DROP INDEX Statement
ALTER TABLE table_name

DROP INDEX index_name;

SQL DESC Statement
DESC table_name;

SQL TRUNCATE TABLE Statement
TRUNCATE TABLE table_name;

SQL ALTER TABLE Statement
ALTER TABLE table_name {ADD|DROP|MODIFY} column_name {data_ype};

SQL ALTER TABLE Statement (Rename)
ALTER TABLE table_name RENAME TO new_table_name;

SQL INSERT INTO Statement
INSERT INTO table_name (column1, column2....columnN)
VALUES (value1, value2....valueN);

SQL UPDATE Statement
UPDATE table_name
SET column1 = value1, column2 = value2....columnN=valueN
[WHERE CONDITION];

SQL DELETE Statement
DELETE FROM table_name
WHERE {CONDITION};

SQL CREATE DATABASE Statement
CREATE DATABASE database_name;

SQL DROP DATABASE Statement
DROP DATABASE database_name;

SQL USE Statement
USE database_name;

SQL COMMIT Statement
COMMIT;

SQL ROLLBACK Statement
ROLLBACK;

The SQL **CREATE DATABASE** statement is used to create a new SQL database.

Syntax

The basic syntax of this CREATE DATABASE statement is as follows.

CREATE DATABASE DatabaseName;

Always the database name should be unique within the RDBMS.

Example

If you want to create a new database <testDB>, then the CREATE DATABASE statement would be as shown below.

SQL> CREATE DATABASE testDB;
SQL> SHOW DATABASES;

```
+--------------------------+
| Database                 |
+--------------------------+
| information_schema       |
| AMROOD                   |
| TUTORIALSPOINT           |
| mysql                    |
| orig                     |
| test                     |
| testDB                   |
+--------------------------+
```

7 rows in set (0.00 sec)

The SQL **DROP DATABASE** statement is used to drop an existing database in SQL schema.

Syntax

The basic syntax of DROP DATABASE statement is as follows.

DROP DATABASE DatabaseName;

Always the database name should be unique within the RDBMS.

Example

SQL> DROP DATABASE testDB;
SQL> SHOW DATABASES;

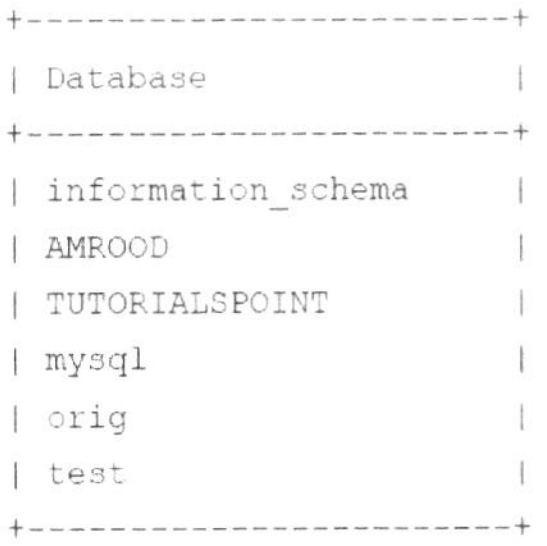

```
+--------------------------+
| Database                 |
+--------------------------+
| information_schema       |
| AMROOD                   |
| TUTORIALSPOINT           |
| mysql                    |
| orig                     |
| test                     |
+--------------------------+
```

6 rows in set (0.00 sec)

The SQL **USE** statement is used to select any existing database in the SQL schema.

Syntax

The basic syntax of the USE statement is as shown below.

USE DatabaseName;

Always the database name should be unique within the RDBMS.

SQL> SHOW DATABASES;

```
+------------------------+
| Database               |
+------------------------+
| information_schema     |
| AMROOD                 |
| TUTORIALSPOINT         |
| mysql                  |
| orig                   |
| test                   |
+------------------------+
```

6 rows in set (0.00 sec)

2.5.   SQL Union

The SQL UNION clause/operator is used to combine the results of two or more SELECT statements without returning any duplicate rows.

To use this UNION clause, each SELECT statement must have,

- The same number of columns selected.
- The same number of column expressions.
- The same data type.
- Have them in the same order.

But they need not have to be in the same length.

Syntax

The basic syntax of a **UNION** clause is as follows:

```
SELECT column1 [, column2]
FROM table1 [, table2]
[WHERE condition]

UNION

SELECT column1 [, column2]
FROM table1 [, table2]
[WHERE condition]
```

Here, the given condition could be any given expression based on your requirement.

Example

Consider the following two tables.

Table 1: CUSTOMERS Table is as Follows

```
+----+----------+-------------+-----------+-----------+
| ID | NAME     | AGE         | ADDRESS   | SALARY |
+----+----------+-------------+-----------+-----------+
| 1  | Ramesh   | 32          | Ahmedabad | 2000.00 |
| 2  | Khilan   | 25          | Delhi     | 1500.00 |
| 3  | kaushik  | 23          | Kota      | 2000.00 |
| 4  | Chaitali | 25          | Mumbai    | 6500.00 |
| 5  | Hardik   | 27          | Bhopal    | 8500.00 |
| 6  | Komal    | 22          | MP        | 4500.00 |
| 7  | Muffy    | 24          | Indore    | 10000.00|
+----+----------+-------------+-----------+-----------+
```

Table 2: ORDERS Table is as Follows

```
+----+----------+-------------+-----------+--------------+
|OID     | DATE                 | CUSTOMER_ID | AMOUNT |
+----+----------+-------------+-----------+--------------+
| 102    | 2009-10-08 00:00:00  | 3           | 3000 |
| 100    | 2009-10-08 00:00:00  | 3           | 1500 |
| 101    | 2009-11-20 00:00:00  | 2           | 1560 |
| 103    | 2008-05-20 00:00:00  | 4           | 2060 |
+----+----------+-------------+-----------+--------------+
```

Now, let us join these two tables in our SELECT statement as follows:

```
SQL> SELECT ID, NAME, AMOUNT, DATE
FROM CUSTOMERS
LEFT JOIN ORDERS
ON CUSTOMERS.ID = ORDERS.CUSTOMER_ID

UNION

SELECT ID, NAME, AMOUNT, DATE
FROM CUSTOMERS
RIGHT JOIN ORDERS
ON CUSTOMERS.ID = ORDERS.CUSTOMER_ID;
```

This would produce the following result.

```
+------+----------+-----------+---------------------+
| ID   | NAME     | AMOUNT    | DATE |
+------+----------+-----------+---------------------+
| 1    | Ramesh   | NULL      | NULL |
| 2    | Khilan   | 1560      | 2009-11-20 00:00:00 |
| 3    | kaushik  | 3000      | 2009-10-08 00:00:00 |
| 3    | kaushik  | 1500      | 2009-10-08 00:00:00 |
| 4    | Chaitali | 2060      | 2008-05-20 00:00:00 |
| 5    | Hardik   | NULL      | NULL |
| 6    | Komal    | NULL      | NULL |
| 7    | Muffy    | NULL      | NULL |
+------+----------+-----------+---------------------+
```

2.6.   SQL Intersect

The SQL **INTERSECT** clause/operator is used to combine two SELECT statements, but returns rows only from the first SELECT statement that are identical to a row in the second SELECT statement. This means INTERSECT returns only common rows returned by the two SELECT statements.

Just as with the UNION operator, the same rules apply when using the INTERSECT operator. MySQL does not support the INTERSECT operator.

Syntax

The basic syntax of **INTERSECT** is as follows.

```
SELECT column1 [, column2]
FROM table1 [, table2]
[WHERE condition]

INTERSECT

SELECT column1 [, column2]
FROM table1 [, table2]
[WHERE condition]
```

Here, the given condition could be any given expression based on your requirement.

Example

Consider the following two tables.

Table 1: CUSTOMERS Table is as Follows

```
+----+----------+-----------------+-----------+----------+
| ID | NAME     | AGE             | ADDRESS   | SALARY |
+----+----------+-----------------+-----------+----------+
| 1  | Ramesh   | 32              | Ahmedabad | 2000.00 |
| 2  | Khilan   | 25              | Delhi     | 1500.00 |
| 3  | kaushik  | 23              | Kota      | 2000.00 |
| 4  | Chaitali | 25              | Mumbai    | 6500.00 |
| 5  | Hardik   | 27              | Bhopal    | 8500.00 |
| 6  | Komal    | 22              | MP        | 4500.00 |
| 7  | Muffy    | 24              | Indore    | 10000.00 |
+----+----------+-----------------+-----------+----------+
```

Table 2: ORDERS Table is as Follows

```
+----+----------+-----------------+-----------+-----------+
|OID       | DATE                    | CUSTOMER_ID  | AMOUNT |
+----+----------+-----------------+-----------+-----------+
| 102      | 2009-10-08 00:00:00     | 3            | 3000 |
| 100      | 2009-10-08 00:00:00     | 3            | 1500 |
| 101      | 2009-11-20 00:00:00     | 2            | 1560 |
| 103      | 2008-05-20 00:00:00     | 4            | 2060 |
+----+----------+-----------------+-----------+-----------+
```

Now, let us join these two tables in our SELECT statement as follows.

```
SQL> SELECT ID, NAME, AMOUNT, DATE
   FROM CUSTOMERS
   LEFT JOIN ORDERS
   ON CUSTOMERS.ID = ORDERS.CUSTOMER_ID

   INTERSECT
   SELECT ID, NAME, AMOUNT, DATE
   FROM CUSTOMERS
   RIGHT JOIN ORDERS
   ON CUSTOMERS.ID = ORDERS.CUSTOMER_ID;
```

This would produce the following result.

```
+------+---------+------------+----------------------+
| ID | NAME      | AMOUNT    | DATE |
+------+---------+------------+----------------------+
| 3  | kaushik   | 3000      | 2009-10-08 00:00:00 |
| 3  | kaushik   | 1500      | 2009-10-08 00:00:00 |
| 2  | Ramesh    | 1560      | 2009-11-20 00:00:00 |
| 4  | kaushik   | 2060      | 2008-05-20 00:00:00 |
+------+---------+------------+----------------------+
```

2.7. SQL Except

The SQL **EXCEPT** clause/operator is used to combine two SELECT statements and returns rows from the first SELECT statement that are not returned by the second SELECT statement. This means EXCEPT returns only rows, which are not available in the second SELECT statement.

Just as with the UNION operator, the same rules apply when using the EXCEPT operator. MySQL does not support the EXCEPT operator.

Syntax

The basic syntax of **EXCEPT** is as follows.

```
SELECT column1 [, column2]
FROM table1 [, table2]
[WHERE condition]


EXCEPT


SELECT column1 [, column2]
FROM table1 [, table2]
[WHERE condition]
```

Here, the given condition could be any given expression based on your requirement.

Example

Consider the following two tables.

Table 1: CUSTOMERS Table is as Follows

```
+------+----------+--------------+---------------------+
| ID | NAME      | AGE          | ADDRESS     | SALARY |
+------+----------+--------------+---------------------+
| 1  | Ramesh    | 32           | Ahmedabad   | 2000.00 |
| 2  | Khilan    | 25           | Delhi       | 1500.00 |
| 3  | kaushik   | 23           | Kota        | 2000.00 |
| 4  | Chaitali  | 25           | Mumbai      | 6500.00 |
| 5  | Hardik    | 27           | Bhopal      | 8500.00 |
| 6  | Komal     | 22           | MP          | 4500.00 |
| 7  | Muffy     | 24           | Indore      | 10000.00|
+------+----------+--------------+---------------------+
```

Table 2: ORDERS Table is as Follows

```
+----------+----------+-------------+---------------------+
|OID       | DATE                    | CUSTOMER_ID | AMOUNT |
+----------+----------+-------------+---------------------+
| 102      | 2009-10-08 00:00:00     | 3           | 3000 |
| 100      | 2009-10-08 00:00:00     | 3           | 1500 |
| 101      | 2009-11-20 00:00:00     | 2           | 1560 |
| 103      | 2008-05-20 00:00:00     | 4           | 2060 |
+----------+----------+-------------+---------------------+
```

Now, let us join these two tables in our SELECT statement as shown below.

```
SQL> SELECT ID, NAME, AMOUNT, DATE
    FROM CUSTOMERS
    LEFT JOIN ORDERS
    ON CUSTOMERS.ID = ORDERS.CUSTOMER_ID


EXCEPT


    SELECT ID, NAME, AMOUNT, DATE
    FROM CUSTOMERS
    RIGHT JOIN ORDERS
    ON CUSTOMERS.ID = ORDERS.CUSTOMER_ID;
```

This would produce the following result.

```
+----+----------+---------+--------------------+
| ID | NAME     | AMOUNT  | DATE               |
+----+----------+---------+--------------------+
|  1 | Ramesh   | NULL    | NULL               |
|  5 | Hardik   | NULL    | NULL               |
|  6 | Komal    | NULL    | NULL               |
|  7 | Muffy    | NULL    | NULL               |
```

2.8. Nested Queries

A Subquery or Inner query or Nested query is a query within another SQL query and embedded within the WHERE clause.

A subquery is used to return data that will be used in the main query as a condition to further restrict the data to be retrieved.

Subqueries can be used with the SELECT, INSERT, UPDATE, and DELETE statements along with the operators like =,, >=, <=, IN, BETWEEN etc.

There are a few rules that subqueries must follow:

Subqueries must be enclosed within parentheses.

A subquery can have only one column in the SELECT clause, unless multiple columns are in the main query for the subquery to compare its selected columns.

An ORDER BY cannot be used in a subquery, although the main query can use an ORDER BY.

The GROUP BY can be used to perform the same function as the ORDER BY in a subquery.

Subqueries that return more than one row can only be used with multiple value operators, such as the IN operator.

The SELECT list cannot include any references to values that evaluate to a BLOB, ARRAY, CLOB, or NCLOB.

A subquery cannot be immediately enclosed in a set function.

The BETWEEN operator cannot be used with a subquery; however, the BETWEEN operator can be used within the subquery.

Subqueries with the SELECT Statement

Subqueries are most frequently used with the SELECT statement.

The basic syntax is as follows:

SELECT column_name [, column_name]

FROM table1 [, table2]

WHERE column_name OPERATOR (SELECT column_name [, column_name] FROM

table1 [, table2] [WHERE])

Example

Consider the CUSTOMERS table having the following records:

```
+----------+----------+----------+-----------------+
| ID | NAME    | AGE  | ADDRESS   | SALARY   |
+----------+----------+----------+-----------------+
| 1  | Ramesh  | 35   | Ahmedabad | 2000.00  |
| 2  | Khilan  | 25   | Delhi     | 1500.00  |
| 3  | kaushik | 23   | Kota      | 2000.00  |
| 4  | Chaitali| 25   | Mumbai    | 6500.00  |
| 5  | Hardik  | 27   | Bhopal    | 8500.00  |
| 6  | Komal   | 22   | MP        | 4500.00  |
| 7  | Muffy   | 24   | Indore    | 10000.00 |
+----------+----------+----------+-----------------+
```

Now, let us check following sub query with SELECT statement:

SQL> SELECT *

FROM CUSTOMERS

WHERE ID IN (SELECT ID

FROM CUSTOMERS

WHERE SALARY > 4500);

This would produce the following result:

```
+----------+----------+----------+-----------------+
| ID | NAME    | AGE  | ADDRESS   | SALARY   |
+----------+----------+----------+-----------------+
| 4  | Chaitali| 25   | Mumbai    | 6500.00  |
| 5  | Hardik  | 27   | Bhopal    | 8500.00  |
| 7  | Muffy   | 24   | Indore    | 10000.00 |
+----------+----------+----------+-----------------+
```

Subqueries with the INSERT Statement

Subqueries also can be used with INSERT statements. The INSERT statement uses the data returned from the subquery to insert into another table. The selected data in the subquery can be modified with any of the character, date or number functions.

The basic syntax is as follows:

INSERT INTO table_name [(column1 [, column2])]

SELECT [*|column1 [, column2]

FROM table1 [, table2] [WHERE VALUE OPERATOR]

Example

Consider a table CUSTOMERS_BKP with similar structure as CUSTOMERS table. Now to copy complete CUSTOMERS table into CUSTOMERS_BKP, following is the syntax:

SQL> INSERT INTO CUSTOMERS_BKP SELECT * FROM CUSTOMERS WHERE ID IN (SELECT ID FROM CUSTOMERS);

Subqueries with the UPDATE Statement

The subquery can be used in conjunction with the UPDATE statement. Either single or multiple columns in a table can be updated when using a subquery with the UPDATE statement.

The basic syntax is as follows:

UPDATE table

SET column_name = new_value [WHERE OPERATOR [VALUE]

(SELECT COLUMN_NAME FROM TABLE_NAME)

[WHERE)]

Example

Assuming, we have CUSTOMERS_BKP table available which is backup of CUSTOMERS table.

Following example updates SALARY by 0.25 times in CUSTOMERS table for all the customers whose AGE is greater than or equal to 27:

SQL> UPDATE CUSTOMERS

SET SALARY = SALARY * 0.25

WHERE AGE IN (SELECT AGE FROM CUSTOMERS_BKP

WHERE AGE >= 27);

This would impact two rows and finally CUSTOMERS table would have the following records:

```
+----------+------------+--------------+---------------------+
| ID | NAME          | AGE          | ADDRESS       | SALARY  |
+----------+------------+--------------+---------------------+
| 1 | Ramesh         | 35           | Ahmedabad     |   125.00 |
| 2 | Khilan         | 25           | Delhi         |  1500.00 |
| 3 | kaushik        | 23           | Kota          |  2000.00 |
| 4 | Chaitali       | 25           | Mumbai        |  6500.00 |
| 5 | Hardik         | 27           | Bhopal        |  2125.00 |
| 6 | Komal          | 22           | MP            |  4500.00 |
| 7 | Muffy          | 24           | Indore        | 10000.00 |
+----------+------------+--------------+---------------------+
```

Subqueries with the DELETE Statement

The subquery can be used in conjunction with the DELETE statement like with any other statements mentioned above.

The basic syntax is as follows:

```
DELETE FROM TABLE_NAME
[WHERE OPERATOR [VALUE] (SELECT COLUMN_NAME FROM TABLE_NAME)
[WHERE)]
```

Example

Assuming, we have CUSTOMERS_BKP table available which is backup of CUSTOMERS table.

Following example deletes records from CUSTOMERS table for all the customers whose AGE is greater than or equal to 27:

```
SQL> DELETE FROM CUSTOMERS
WHERE AGE IN (SELECT AGE FROM CUSTOMERS_BKP
WHERE AGE > 27);
```

This would impact two rows and finally CUSTOMERS table would have the following records:

```
+----------+------------+--------------+---------------------+
| ID | NAME          | AGE          | ADDRESS | SALARY  |
+----------+------------+--------------+---------------------+
| 2  | Khilan        | 25           | Delhi   | 1500.00 |
| 3  | kaushik       | 23           | Kota    | 2000.00 |
| 4  | Chaitali      | 25           | Mumbai  | 6500.00 |
| 6  | Komal         | 22           | MP      | 4500.00 |
| 7  | Muffy         | 24           | Indore  | 10000.00 |
+----------+------------+--------------+---------------------+
```

2.9.   Aggregate Operators

Aggregate functions in DBMS take multiple rows from the table and return a value according to the query.

All the aggregate functions are used in Select statement.

Syntax

SELECT <FUNCTION NAME> (<PARAMETER>) FROM <TABLE NAME>

AVG Function

This function returns the average value of the numeric column that is supplied as a parameter.

Example: Write a query to select average salary from employee table.

Select AVG (salary) from Employee.

COUNT Function

The count function returns the number of rows in the result. It does not count the null values.

Example: Write a query to return number of rows where salary > 20000.

Select COUNT (*) from Employee where Salary > 20000;

Types:

- COUNT (*): Counts all the number of rows of the table including null.
- COUNT (COLUMN_NAME): count number of non-null values in column.
- COUNT (DISTINCT COLUMN_NAME): count number of distinct values in a column.

MAX Function

The MAX function is used to find maximum value in the column that is supplied as a parameter. It can be used on any type of data.

Example: Write a query to find the maximum salary in employee table.

Select MAX (salary) from Employee.

SUM Function

This function sums up the values in the column supplied as a parameter.

Example: Write a query to get the total salary of employees.

Select SUM (salary) from Employee.

STDDEV Function

The STDDEV function is used to find standard deviation of the column specified as argument.

Example: Write a query to find standard deviation of salary in Employee table.

Select STDDEV (salary) from Employee.

VARIANCE Function

The VARIANCE Function is used to find variance of the column specified as argument.

Example

Select VARIANCE (salary) from Employee.

2.10. NULL Values

The SQL **NULL** is the term used to represent a missing value. A NULL value in a table is a value in a field that appears to be blank.

A field with a NULL value is a field with no value. It is very important to understand that a NULL value is different than a zero value or a field that contains spaces.

Syntax

The basic syntax of **NULL** while creating a table.

```
SQL> CREATE TABLE CUSTOMERS (
 ID INT NOT NULL,
 NAME VARCHAR (20) NOT NULL,
 AGE INT NOT NULL,
 ADDRESS CHAR (25),
 SALARY DECIMAL (18, 2),
 PRIMARY KEY (ID)
 );
```

Here, **NOT NULL** signifies that column should always accept an explicit value of the given data type. There are two columns where we did not use NOT NULL, which means these columns could be NULL.

A field with a NULL value is the one that has been left blank during the record creation.

Example

The NULL value can cause problems when selecting data. However, because when comparing an unknown value to any other value, the result is always unknown and not included in the results. You must use the **IS NULL** or **IS NOT NULL** operators to check for a NULL value.

Consider the following CUSTOMERS table having the records as shown below.

```
+----------+----------+-------------+---------------------+
| ID | NAME         | AGE       | ADDRESS       | SALARY |
+----------+----------+-------------+---------------------+
| 1  | Ramesh       | 32        | Ahmedabad     | 2000.00 |
| 2  | Khilan       | 25        | Delhi         | 1500.00 |
| 3  | kaushik      | 23        | Kota          | 2000.00 |
| 4  | Chaitali     | 25        | Mumbai        | 6500.00 |
| 5  | Hardik       | 27        | Bhopal        | 8500.00 |
| 6  | Komal        | 22        | MP            |         |
| 7  | Muffy        | 24        | Indore        |         |
+----------+----------+-------------+---------------------+
```

Now, following is the usage of the **IS NOT NULL** operator.

```
SQL> SELECT ID, NAME, AGE, ADDRESS, SALARY
     FROM CUSTOMERS
     WHERE SALARY IS NOT NULL;
```

This would produce the following result:

```
+----------+----------+-------------+---------------------+
| ID | NAME         | AGE       | ADDRESS       | SALARY |
+----------+----------+-------------+---------------------+
| 1  | Ramesh       | 32        | Ahmedabad     | 2000.00 |
| 2  | Khilan       | 25        | Delhi         | 1500.00 |
| 3  | kaushik      | 23        | Kota          | 2000.00 |
| 4  | Chaitali     | 25        | Mumbai        | 6500.00 |
| 5  | Hardik       | 27        | Bhopal        | 8500.00 |
+----------+----------+-------------+---------------------+
```

Now, following is the usage of the **IS NULL** operator.

```
SQL> SELECT ID, NAME, AGE, ADDRESS, SALARY
     FROM CUSTOMERS
     WHERE SALARY IS NULL;
```

This would produce the following result.

```
+----------+----------+--------------+----------+
| ID | NAME    | AGE    | ADDRESS     | SALARY  |
+----------+----------+--------------+----------+
| 6  | Komal   | 22     | MP          |         |
| 7  | Muffy   | 24     | Indore      |         |
+----------+----------+--------------+----------+
```

2.11. Complex Integrity Constraints in SQL

Constraints are the rules enforced on the data columns of a table. These are used to limit the type of data that can go into a table. This ensures the accuracy and reliability of the data in the database.

Constraints could be either on a column level or a table level. The column level constraints are applied only to one column, whereas the table level constraints are applied to the whole table.

Following are some of the most commonly used constraints available in SQL. These constraints have already been discussed in SQL - RDBMS Concepts chapter, but its worth to revise them at this point.

- **NOT NULL Constraint** – Ensures that a column cannot have NULL value.
- **DEFAULT Constraint** – Provides a default value for a column when none is specified.
- **UNIQUE Constraint** – Ensures that all values in a column are different.
- **PRIMARY Key** – Uniquely identifies each row/record in a database table.
- **FOREIGN Key** – Uniquely identifies a row/record in any of the given database table.
- **CHECK Constraint** – The CHECK constraint ensures that all the values in a column satisfies certain conditions.
- **INDEX** – Used to create and retrieve data from the database very quickly.

Constraints can be specified when a table is created with the CREATE TABLE statement or you can use the ALTER TABLE statement to create constraints even after the table is created.

Dropping Constraints

Any constraint that you have defined can be dropped using the ALTER TABLE command with the DROP CONSTRAINT option.

For example, to drop the primary key constraint in the EMPLOYEES table, you can use the following command.

ALTER TABLE EMPLOYEES DROP CONSTRAINT EMPLOYEES_PK;

Some implementations may provide shortcuts for dropping certain constraints. For example, to drop the primary key constraint for a table in Oracle, you can use the following command.

ALTER TABLE EMPLOYEES DROP PRIMARY KEY;

Some implementations allow you to disable constraints. Instead of permanently dropping a constraint from the database, you may want to temporarily disable the constraint and then enable it later.

Integrity Constraints

Integrity constraints are used to ensure accuracy and consistency of the data in a relational database. Data integrity is handled in a relational database through the concept of referential integrity.

There are many types of integrity constraints that play a role in **Referential Integrity (RI)**. These constraints include Primary Key, Foreign Key, Unique Constraints and other constraints which are mentioned above.

2.12. Triggers and Active Data Bases

Triggers can be defined on the table, view, schema, or database with which the event is associated.

Benefits of Triggers

Triggers can be written for the following purposes:

- Generating some derived column values automatically.
- Enforcing referential integrity.
- Event logging and storing information on table access.
- Auditing.
- Synchronous replication of tables.
- Imposing security authorizations.
- Preventing invalid transactions.

Creating Triggers

The syntax for creating a trigger is,

```
CREATE [OR REPLACE] TRIGGER trigger_name
{BEFORE | AFTER | INSTEAD OF}
{INSERT [OR] | UPDATE [OR] | DELETE}
[OF col_name]
ON table_name
[REFERENCING OLD AS o NEW AS n]
[FOR EACH ROW]
WHEN (condition)
DECLARE
   Declaration-statements
BEGIN
   Executable-statements
EXCEPTION
   Exception-handling-statements
END;
```

Where,

- CREATE [OR REPLACE] TRIGGER trigger_name – Creates or replaces an existing trigger with the *trigger_name*.
- {BEFORE | AFTER | INSTEAD OF} – This specifies when the trigger will be executed. The INSTEAD OF clause is used for creating trigger on a view.
- {INSERT [OR] | UPDATE [OR] | DELETE} – This specifies the DML operation.
- [OF col_name] – This specifies the column name that will be updated.
- [ON table_name] – This specifies the name of the table associated with the trigger.
- [REFERENCING OLD AS o NEW AS n] – This allows you to refer new and old values for various DML statements, such as INSERT, UPDATE, and DELETE.
- [FOR EACH ROW] – This specifies a row-level trigger, i.e., the trigger will be executed for each row being affected. Otherwise the trigger will execute just once when the SQL statement is executed, which is called a table level trigger.
- WHEN (condition) – This provides a condition for rows for which the trigger would fire. This clause is valid only for row-level triggers.

Example

To start with, we will be using the CUSTOMERS table we had created and used in the previous chapters:

Select * from customers;

```
+----------+-----------+-------------+-------------   +
| ID | NAME           | AGE       | ADDRESS      | SALARY |
+----------+-----------+-------------+----------------+
| 1  | Ramesh         | 32        | Ahmedabad    | 2000.00 |
| 2  | Khilan         | 25        | Delhi        | 1500.00 |
| 3  | kaushik        | 23        | Kota         | 2000.00 |
| 4  | Chaitali       | 25        | Mumbai       | 6500.00 |
| 5  | Hardik         | 27        | Bhopal       | 8500.00 |
| 6  | Komal          | 22        | MP           | 4500.00 |
+----------+-----------+-------------+----------------+
```

The following program creates a **row-level** trigger for the customers table that would fire for INSERT or UPDATE or DELETE operations performed on the CUSTOMERS table. This trigger will display the salary difference between the old values and new values.

```
CREATE OR REPLACE TRIGGER display_salary_changes
BEFORE DELETE OR INSERT OR UPDATE ON customers
FOR EACH ROW
WHEN (NEW.ID > 0)
DECLARE
    sal_diff number;
BEGIN
   sal_diff := :NEW.salary - :OLD.salary;
   dbms_output.put_line('Old salary: ' || :OLD.salary);
   dbms_output.put_line('New salary: ' || :NEW.salary);
   dbms_output.put_line('Salary difference: ' || sal_diff);
END;
/
```

When the above code is executed at the SQL prompt, it produces the following result:

Trigger created.

The following points need to be considered here:

- OLD and NEW references are not available for table-level triggers, rather you can use them for record-level triggers.

- If you want to query the table in the same trigger, then you should use the AFTER keyword, because triggers can query the table or change it again only after the initial changes are applied and the table is back in a consistent state.

- The above trigger has been written in such a way that it will fire before any DELETE or INSERT or UPDATE operation on the table, but you can write your trigger on a single or multiple operations, for example BEFORE DELETE, which will fire whenever a record will be deleted using the DELETE operation on the table.

Triggering a Trigger

Let us perform some DML operations on the CUSTOMERS table. Here is one INSERT statement, which will create a new record in the table.

```
INSERT INTO CUSTOMERS (ID,NAME,AGE,ADDRESS,SALARY)
VALUES (7, 'Kriti', 22, 'HP', 7500.00);
```

When a record is created in the CUSTOMERS table, the above create trigger, **display_salary_changes** will be fired and it will display the following result.

```
Old salary:
New salary: 7500
Salary difference:
```

Because this is a new record, old salary is not available and the above result comes as null. Let us now perform one more DML operation on the CUSTOMERS table. The UPDATE statement will update an existing record in the table.

```
UPDATE customers
SET salary = salary + 500
WHERE id = 2;
```

When a record is updated in the CUSTOMERS table, the above create trigger, **display_salary_changes** will be fired and it will display the following result.

```
Old salary: 1500
New salary: 2000
Salary difference: 500
```

2.13. Designing Active Data Bases

A database that has the ability to spontaneously react to events occurring inside as well as outside the system is called active database. The ability to respond to external events is called active behaviour. The active behaviour is based on the rules that integrate a event with the desired effect. This behaviour is commonly defined in terms of ECA rules allowing system to react to specific events.

Active Rules (Production Rules)

The active behaviour is achieved through the production rules/ active rules.

The active rules are stored programs called triggers that are fired when an event occurs.

Triggers are written to respond to DML (select, insert etc), DDL (create, alter etc) and Database Operations (Log-On, Log-Off).

These triggers can be defined on table/view or the database to which event is associated.

Architecture

The architecture depends on the knowledge model and execution model Knowledge model for triggers:

- What kind of rules will be supported?
    - What these rules are?
    - Classification of rules at security levels.
    - Execution model.
- Specify runtime strategy for rule execution
    - Ensure that no illegal information should flow due.
    - Execution of a trigger.

There are two types of architecture for active databases:

- Built-in Architecture.
- Layered Architecture.

Built-In Architecture

Active database components become part of database. Can be achieved by two models:

- **Implementation from scratch:** Active components are implemented as a part of database from scratch.

- **Integrated Architecture:** This involves modifying and extending the existing passive database.

    1. **Event Detector:** It detects any external event occurring and informs the condition manager about it.

    2. **Condition Monitor:** It evaluates the conditions of rules associated with events that have been detected by the event detector.

    3. **Scheduler:** It compares recently triggered rules with those that have previously been triggered, updates the conflict set, and fires any rules that are scheduled for immediate processing.

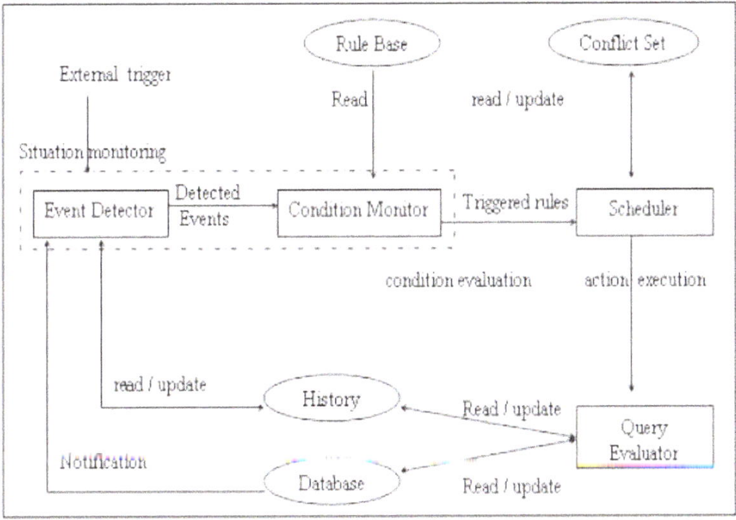

    4. **Query Evaluator:** It executes database queries or actions. Access may be required both to the current state of database and to past states in order to support monitoring of how the database is evolving.

2.14. Layered Architecture

Active database components are built on top of existing passive database system. Layered approach is better for active object oriented database when base system is object oriented database, as it allows reusability of constructed rules for other tables/databases. It is easier to modify the rules according to the evolving needs.

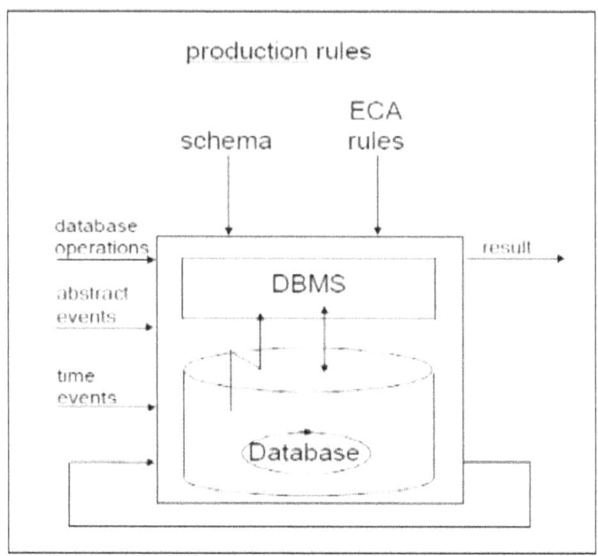

As evident from the diagram the active rules are implemented on the top of existing database.

Features

- All the features of a conventional database apply to active database too.
- Support ECA rules.
- Detect the occurrence of events.
- Evaluate conditions to execute actions.
- Support programming environment.

Advantages

- The triggering capabilities enhance the functionalities of traditional database.
- Same event-driven rules can be applied to every relevant operation of an organization.
- Triggers can improve the working of a database by removing repetitive error check and correction.
- The inference power of ECA rules makes active database systems a suitable platform for building large and efficient knowledge base and expert systems.

The ECA rules help in:

- Enforcing integrity constraints.
- Implement version control policies.
- Implement triggers and alert systems.
- Enforce access constraints.
- Gather statistics for query optimization.

Disadvantages

- Lack of standardization.
- Has been mostly implemented for centralized dbms.
- Distributed, parallel dbms has not been considered.
- The layered approach is beneficial in terms of construction cost, but the entire system cannot be optimized comprehensively and this degrades runtime performance.
- Optimizing large applications is rendered difficult by the separation of transactions and triggers and the misunderstanding of their fine-drawn interactions.

Applications

- Production control e.g. Power plants.
- Maintenance tasks.
- Share trading.
- Air Traffic control.
- Statistics gathering and authorization tools.

3. Schema Refinement and Normal Forms

3.1.   Introduction to Schema Refinement

Schema refinement is just a fancy term for saying **polishing tables**. It is the last step before considering physical design/tuning with typical workloads:

- **Requirement analysis:** User needs.

- **Conceptual design:** High-level description, often using E/R diagrams.

- **Logical design:** From graphs to tables (relational schema).

- **Schema refinement:** Checking tables for redundancies and anomalies.

Let's see an example of redundancies and anomalies. Consider the following table where the client's name is the primary key.

employeeID	FirstName	LastName	Hire Date	Client
1	Mary	Marley	1/1/2005	James H.
2	Robert	Crosby	2/4/2008	Clark L.
3	Robert	Crosby	2/4/2008	Tina M.

The table is presenting information on employees (sales reps) and their clients.

If we want to **insert data**, we notice that:

- each row requires an entry in the client field.

- we can't insert data for newly hired sales reps until they've been assigned to one or more clients.

- if sales reps are in a training process, even if they've been already hired, they can't actually join the database because they need to have a delegated client... unless "dummy" clients are created.

If we want to **update data**, we notice that:

- The sales reps name is repeated for each client.

- What if, for a given client, we misspelled the name of the sales reps Crosby instead of Cosby... how can we edit that without affecting all the sales reps called Crosby?

If we want to **delete data**, what if Mary doesn't have a client anymore because she's taking a year off? We are forced to either.

- Create a dummy client.

- Incorrectly showing her with a client she no longer handled.

- Delete Mary's record (even if however she's still an employee).

- Notice we cannot have "null" as a client since primary field keys cannot store null.

When we have to treat with **schema refinement** we often notice that the main problem is **redundancy**. In order to identify schemas with such problems, we'll introduce the notion of **functional dependencies**: a relationship that exists when one attribute uniquely determines another attribute. A **functional dependency** is simply a new type of constraint between two attributes.

Say that R is a relation with attributes X and Y, we say that there is a functional dependency X -> Y when **Y is functionally dependent on X** (where X is the **determinant set** and Y is the **dependent attribute**).

Let's illustrate a scenario where the designer didn't take in consideration dependencies between columns.

- Data (studID, studName, address, courseID, courseName, grade).

The following structure is considerably better:

- Student (studID, studName, address).

- Course (courseID, courseName).

- Enrolled (studID, courseID, grade).

Functional Dependencies

Functional Dependency is when one attribute determines another attribute in a DBMS system. Functional Dependency plays a vital role to find the difference between good and bad database design.

Example

Employee number	Employee Name	Salary	City
1	Dana	50000	San Francisco
2	Francis	38000	London
3	Andrew	25000	Tokyo

In this example, if we know the value of Employee number, we can obtain Employee Name, city, salary, etc.

By this, we can say that the city, Employee Name, and salary are functionally depended on Employee number.

A functional dependency is denoted by an arrow →

The functional dependency of X on Y is represented by X →Y

Here, are some key terms for functional dependency:

Key Terms	Description
Axiom	Axioms is a set of inference rules used to infer all the functional dependencies on a relational database.
Decomposition	It is a rule that suggests if you have a table that appears to contain two entities which are determined by the same primary key then you should consider breaking them up into two different tables.
Dependent	It is displayed on the right side of the functional dependency diagram.
Determinant	It is displayed on the left side of the functional dependency Diagram.
Union	It suggests that if two tables are separate, and the PK is the same, you should consider putting them. Together.

Rules of Functional Dependencies

Below given are the Three most important rules for Functional Dependency:

- **Reflexive rule:** If X is a set of attributes and Y is_subset_of X, then X holds a value of Y.
- **Augmentation rule:** When x -> y holds, and c is attribute set, then ac -> bc also holds. That is adding attributes which do not change the basic dependencies.
- **Transitivity rule:** This rule is very much similar to the transitive rule in algebra if x -> y holds and y -> z holds, then x -> z also holds. X -> y is called as functionally that determines y.

Types of Functional Dependencies

- Multivalued dependency.
- Trivial functional dependency.
- Non-trivial functional dependency.
- Transitive dependency.

Multivalued Dependency in DBMS

Multivalued dependency occurs in the situation where there are multiple independent multivalued attributes in a single table. A multivalued dependency is a complete constraint between two sets of attributes in a relation. It requires that certain tuples be present in a relation.

Example

Car_model	Maf_year	Color
H001	2017	Metallic
H001	2017	Green
H005	2018	Metallic
H005	2018	Blue
H010	2015	Metallic
H033	2012	Gray

In this example, maf_year and color are independent of each other but dependent on car_model. In this example, these two columns are said to be multivalue dependent on car_model.

This dependence can be represented like this:

car_model -> maf_year

car_model-> colour

Trivial Functional Dependency

The Trivial dependency is a set of attributes which are called a trivial if the set of attributes are included in that attribute.

So, X -> Y is a trivial functional dependency if Y is a subset of X.

For Example

Emp_id	Emp_name
AS555	Harry
AS811	George
AS999	Kevin

Consider this table with two columns Emp_id and Emp_name.

{Emp_id, Emp_name} -> Emp_id is a trivial functional dependency as Emp_id is a subset of {Emp_id, Emp_name}.

Non Trivial Functional Dependency in DBMS

Functional dependency which also known as a nontrivial dependency occurs when A->B holds true where B is not a subset of A. In a relationship, if attribute B is not a subset of attribute A, then it is considered as a non-trivial dependency.

Company	CEO	Age
Microsoft	Satya Nadella	51
Google	Sundar Pichai	46
Apple	Tim Cook	57

Example

{Company} -> {CEO} (if we know the Company, we knows the CEO name).

But CEO is not a subset of Company, and hence it's non-trivial functional dependency.

Transitive Dependency

A transitive is a type of functional dependency which happens when t is indirectly formed by two functional dependencies.

Example

Company	CEO	Age
Microsoft	Satya Nadella	51
Google	Sundar Pichai	46
Alibaba	Jack Ma	54

{Company} -> {CEO} (if we know the compay, we know its CEO's name).

{CEO} -> {Age} If we know the CEO, we know the Age.

Therefore according to the rule of rule of transitive dependency:

{Company} -> {Age} should hold, that makes sense because if we know the company name, we can know his age.

Note: You need to remember that transitive dependency can only occur in a relation of three or more attributes.

Normal Forms

Normalization is a method of organizing the data in the database which helps you to avoid data redundancy, insertion, update & deletion anomaly. It is a process of analyzing the relation schemas based on their different functional dependencies and primary key.

Normalization is inherent to relational database theory. It may have the effect of duplicating the same data within the database which may result in the creation of additional tables.

Advantages of Functional Dependency

- Functional Dependency avoids data redundancy. Therefore same data do not repeat at multiple locations in that database.
- It helps you to maintain the quality of data in the database.
- It helps you to defined meanings and constraints of databases.
- It helps you to identify bad designs.
- It helps you to find the facts regarding the database design.

Reasoning about FDs

Inference Rule (IR):

- The Armstrong's axioms are the basic inference rule.
- Armstrong's axioms are used to conclude functional dependencies on a relational database.
- The inference rule is a type of assertion. It can apply to a set of FD (functional dependency) to derive other FD.
- Using the inference rule, we can derive additional functional dependency from the initial set.

The Functional dependency has 6 types of inference rule:

1. Reflexive Rule (IR₁)

In the reflexive rule, if Y is a subset of X, then X determines Y.

If $X \supseteq Y$ then $X \rightarrow Y$

Example

$X = \{a, b, c, d, e\}$

$Y = \{a, b, c\}$

2. Augmentation Rule (IR₂)

The augmentation is also called as a partial dependency. In augmentation, if X determines Y, then XZ determines YZ for any Z.

If $X \rightarrow Y$ then $XZ \rightarrow YZ$

Example

For R(ABCD), **if** $A \rightarrow B$ then $AC \rightarrow BC$

3. Transitive Rule (IR₃)

In the transitive rule, if X determines Y and Y determine Z, then X must also determine Z.

If $X \rightarrow Y$ and $Y \rightarrow Z$ then $X \rightarrow Z$

4. Union Rule (IR₄)

Union rule says, if X determines Y and X determines Z, then X must also determine Y and Z.

If $X \rightarrow Y$ and $X \rightarrow Z$ then $X \rightarrow YZ$

Proof

X → Y (given)

X → Z (given)

X → XY (using IR_2 on 1 by augmentation with X. Where XX = X)

XY → YZ (using IR_2 on 2 by augmentation with Y)

X → YZ (using IR_3 on 3 and 4)

5. Decomposition Rule (IR_5)

Decomposition rule is also known as project rule. It is the reverse of union rule.

This Rule says, if X determines Y and Z, then X determines Y and X determines Z separately.

If X → YZ then X → Y and X → Z

Proof

X → YZ (given)

YZ → Y (using IR_1 Rule)

X → Y (using IR_3 on 1 and 2)

6. Pseudo Transitive Rule (IR_6)

In Pseudo transitive Rule, if X determines Y and YZ determines W, then XZ determines W.

If X → Y and YZ → W then XZ → W

Proof

X → Y (given)

WY → Z (given)

WX → WY (using IR_2 on 1 by augmenting with W)

WX → Z (using IR_3 on 3 and 2)

Normal Forms

Normalization

- Normalization is the process of organizing the data in the database.
- Normalization is used to minimize the redundancy from a relation or set of relations. It is also used to eliminate the undesirable characteristics like Insertion, Update and Deletion Anomalies.
- Normalization divides the larger table into the smaller table and links them using relationship.
- The normal form is used to reduce redundancy from the database table.

Types of Normal Forms

There are the four types of normal forms:

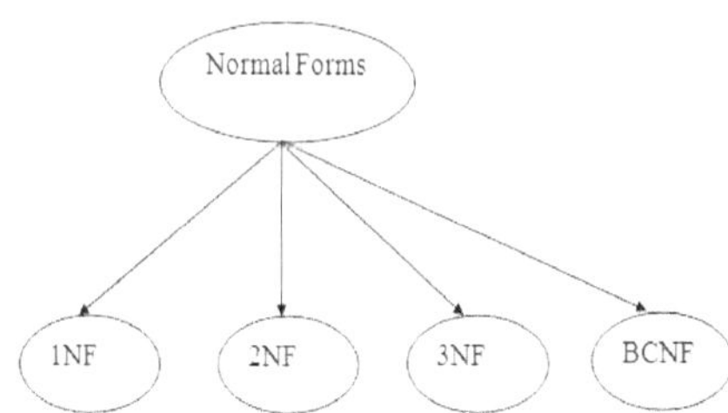

Normal Form	Description
1NF	A relation is in 1NF if it contains an atomic value.
2NF	A relation will be in 2NF if it is in 1NF and all non-key attributes are fully functional dependent on the primary key.
3NF	A relation will be in 3NF if it is in 2NF and no transition dependency exists.
4NF	A relation will be in 4NF if it is in Boyce Codd normal form and has no multi-valued dependency.
5NF	A relation is in 5NF if it is in 4NF and not contains any join dependency and joining should be lossless.

Properties of Decompositions

- Decomposition is the process of breaking down in parts or elements.

- It replaces a relation with a collection of smaller relations.

- It breaks the table into multiple tables in a database.

- It should always be lossless, because it confirms that the information in the original relation can be accurately reconstructed based on the decomposed relations.

- If there is no proper decomposition of the relation, then it may lead to problems like loss of information.

Properties of Decomposition

Following are the properties of Decomposition.

- Lossless Decomposition

- Dependency Preservation

- Lack of Data Redundancy

1. Lossless Decomposition

- Decomposition must be lossless. It means that the information should not get lost from the relation that is decomposed.

- It gives a guarantee that the join will result in the same relation as it was decomposed.

Example

- Let's take 'E' is the Relational Schema, With instance 'e'; is decomposed into: E1, E2, E3, ... En; With instance: e1, e2, e3, ... en, If e1 ⋈ e2 ⋈ e3 . . . . ⋈ en, then it is called as **'Lossless Join Decomposition'**.

- In the above example, it means that, if natural joins of all the decomposition give the original relation, then it is said to be lossless join decomposition.

Example: <Employee_Department> Table

Eid	Ename	Age	City	Salary	Deptid	DeptName
E001	ABC	29	Pune	20000	D001	Finance
E002	PQR	30	Pune	30000	D002	Production
E003	LMN	25	Mumbai	5000	D003	Sales
E004	XYZ	24	Mumbai	4000	D004	Marketing
E005	STU	32	Bangalore	25000	D005	Human Resource

- Decompose the above relation into two relations to check whether a decomposition is lossless or lossy.

- Now, we have decomposed the relation that is Employee and Department.

Relation 1: <Employee> Table

Eid	Ename	Age	City	Salary
E001	ABC	29	Pune	20000
E002	PQR	30	Pune	30000
E003	LMN	25	Mumbai	5000
E004	XYZ	24	Mumbai	4000
E005	STU	32	Bangalore	25000

- Employee Schema contains (Eid, Ename, Age, City, Salary).

Relation 2: <Department> Table

Deptid	Eid	DeptName
D001	E001	Finance
D002	E002	Production
D003	E003	Sales
D004	E004	Marketing
D005	E005	Human Resource

- Department Schema contains (Deptid, Eid, DeptName).

- So, the above decomposition is a Lossless Join Decomposition, because the two relations contains one common field that is 'Eid' and therefore join is possible.

- Now apply natural join on the decomposed relations.

Employee ⋈ Department

Eid	Ename	Age	City	Salary	Deptid	DeptName
E001	ABC	29	Pune	20000	D001	Finance
E002	PQR	30	Pune	30000	D002	Production
E003	LMN	25	Mumbai	5000	D003	Sales
E004	XYZ	24	Mumbai	4000	D004	Marketing
E005	STU	32	Bangalore	25000	D005	Human Resource

Hence, the decomposition is Lossless Join Decomposition.

- If the <Employee> table contains (Eid, Ename, Age, City, Salary) and <Department> table contains (Deptid and DeptName), then it is not possible to join the two tables or relations, because there is no common column between them. And it becomes **Lossy Join Decomposition.**

2. Dependency Preservation

- Dependency is an important constraint on the database.

- Every dependency must be satisfied by at least one decomposed table.

- If $\{A \rightarrow B\}$ holds, then two sets are functional dependent. And, it becomes more useful for checking the dependency easily if both sets in a same relation.

- This decomposition property can only be done by maintaining the functional dependency.

- In this property, it allows to check the updates without computing the natural join of the database structure.

3. Lack of Data Redundancy

- Lack of Data Redundancy is also known as a **Repetition of Information.**

- The proper decomposition should not suffer from any data redundancy.

- The careless decomposition may cause a problem with the data.

- The lack of data redundancy property may be achieved by Normalization process.

Normalization is a process of organizing the data in the database.

- It is a systematic approach of decomposing tables to eliminate data redundancy.
- It was developed by **E. F. Codd.**
- Normalization is a multi-step process that puts the data into a tabular form by removing the duplicate data from the relation tables.
- It is a step by step decomposition of complex records into simple records.
- It is also called as Canonical Synthesis.
- It is the technique of building database structures to store data.

Definition of Normalization

"Normalization is a process of designing a consistent database by minimizing redundancy and ensuring data integrity through decomposition which is lossless."

Features of Normalization

- Normalization avoids the data redundancy.
- It is a formal process of developing data structures.
- It promotes the data integrity.
- It ensures data dependencies make sense that means data is logically stored.
- It eliminates the undesirable characteristics like Insertion, Updation and Deletion Anomalies.

Types of Normalization

Following are the types of Normalization:

- First Normal Form
- Second Normal Form
- Third Normal Form
- Fourth Normal Form
- Fifth Normal Form
- BCNF (Boyce – Codd Normal Form)
- DKNF (Domain Key Normal Form)

1. First Normal Form (1NF)

- First Normal Form (1NF) is a simple form of Normalization.
- It simplifies each attribute in a relation.

- In 1NF, there should not be any repeating group of data.

- Each set of column must have a unique value.

- It contains atomic values because the table cannot hold multiple values.

Example: Employee Table

ECode	Employee_Name	Department_Name
1	ABC	Sales, Production
2	PQR	Human Resource
3	XYZ	Quality Assurance, Marketing

Employee Table using 1NF

ECode	Employee_Name	Department_Name
1	ABC	Sales
1	ABC	Production
2	PQR	Human Resource
3	XYZ	Quality Assurance
3	XYZ	Marketing

2. Second Normal Form (2NF)

- In 2NF, the table is required in 1NF.

- The main rule of 2NF is, 'No non-prime attribute is dependent on the proper subset of any candidate key of the table.'

- An attribute which is not part of candidate key is known as non-prime attribute.

Example: Employee Table using 1NF

ECode	Employee_Name	Employee_Age
1	ABC	38
1	ABC	38
2	PQR	38
3	XYZ	40
3	XYZ	40

Candidate Key: ECode, Employee_Name

Non prime attribute: Employee_Age

The above table is in 1NF. Each attribute has atomic values. However, it is not in 2NF because non prime attribute Employee_Age is dependent on ECode alone, which is a proper subset of candidate key. This violates the rule for 2NF as the rule says 'No non-prime attribute is dependent on the proper subset of any candidate key of the table'.

2NF (Second Normal Form): Employee1 Table

ECode	Employee_Age
1	38
2	38
3	40

Employee 2 Table

ECode	Employee_Name
1	ABC
1	ABC
2	PQR
3	XYZ
3	XYZ

Now, the above tables comply with the Second Normal Form (2NF).

3. Third Normal Form (3NF)

- Third Normal Form (3NF) is used to minimize the transitive redundancy.

- In 3NF, the table is required in 2NF.

- While using the 2NF table, there should not be any transitive partial dependency.

- 3NF reduces the duplication of data and also achieves the data integrity.

Example: <Employee> Table

EId	Ename	DOB	City	State	Zip
001	ABC	10/05/1990	Pune	Maharashtra	411038
002	XYZ	11/05/1988	Mumbai	Maharashtra	400007

- In the above <Employee> table, EId is a primary key but City, State depends upon Zip code.

- The dependency between Zip and other fields is called Transitive Dependency.

- Therefore we apply 3NF. So, we need to move the city and state to the new <Employee_Table2> table, with Zip as a Primary key.

<Employee_Table1> Table

EId	Ename	DOB	Zip
001	ABC	10/05/1990	411038
002	XYZ	11/05/1988	400007

<Employee_Table2> Table

City	State	Zip
Pune	Maharashtra	411038
Mumbai	Maharashtra	400007

- The advantage of removing transitive dependency is, it reduces the amount of data dependencies and achieves the data integrity.

- In the above example, using with the 3NF, there is no redundancy of data while inserting the new records.

- The City, State and Zip code will be stored in the separate table. And therefore the updation becomes more easier because of no data redundancy.

4. BCNF (Boyce – Code Normal Form)

- BCNF which stands for Boyce – Code Normal From is developed by Raymond F. Boyce and E. F. Codd in 1974.

- BCNF is a higher version of 3NF.

- It deals with the certain type of anomaly which is not handled by 3NF.

- A table complies with BCNF if it is in 3NF and any attribute is fully functionally dependent that is A → B. (Attribute 'A' is determinant).

- If every determinant is a candidate key, then it is said to be BCNF.

- Candidate key has the ability to become a primary key. It is a column in a table.

Example: <Employee Main> Table

Empid	Ename	DeptName	DeptType
E001	ABC	Production	D001
E002	XYZ	Sales	D002

The functional dependencies are:

Empid → EmpName

DeptName → DeptType

Candidate Key

Empid

DeptName

- The above table is not in BCNF as neither Empid nor DeptName alone are keys.

- We can break the table in three tables to make it comply with BCNF.

<Employee> Table

Empid	EmpName
E001	ABC
E002	XYZ

<Department> Table

DeptName	DeptType
Production	D001
Sales	D002

<Emp_Dept> Table

Empid	DeptName
E001	Production
E002	Sales

Now, the functional dependencies are:

Empid → EmpName

DeptName → DeptType

Candidate Key

<Employee> Table: Empid

<Department> Table: DeptType

<Emp_Dept> Table: Empid, DeptType

So, now both the functional dependencies left side part is a key, so it is in the BCNF.

5. Fourth Normal Form (4NF)

- Fourth Normal Form (4NF) does not have non-trivial multivalued dependencies other than a candidate key.

- 4NF builds on the first three normal forms (1NF, 2NF and 3NF) and the BCNF.

- It does not contain more than one multivalued dependency.

- This normal form is rarely used outside of academic circles.

For example: A table contains a list of three things that is 'Student', 'Teacher', and 'Book'. Teacher is in charge of Student and recommended book for each student. These three elements (Student, Teacher and Book) are independent of one another. Changing the student's recommended book, for instance, has no effect on the student itself. This is an example of multivalued dependency, where an item depends on more than one value. In this example, the student depends on both teacher and book.

Therefore, 4NF states that a table should not have more than one dependency.

6. Fifth Normal Form (5NF)

- 5NF is also knows as Project-Join Normal Form (PJ/NF).

- It is designed for reducing the redundancy in relational databases.

- 5NF requires semantically related multiple relationships, which are rare.

- In 5NF, if an attribute is multivalued attribute, then it must be taken out as a separate entity.

- While performing 5NF, the table must be in 4NF.

7. DKNF (Domain Key Normal Form)

- DKNF stands for Domain Key Normal Form requires the database that contains no constraints other than domain constraints and key constraints.

- In DKNF, it is easy to build a database.

- It avoids general constraints in the database which are not clear domain or key constraints.

- The 3NF, 4NF, 5NF and BCNF are special cases of the DKNF.

- It is achieved when every constraint on the relation is a logical consequence of the definition.

3.2.   Schema Refinement in Database Design

A **functional dependency** is simply a new type of constraint between two attributes.

Say that R is a relation with attributes X and Y, we say that there is a functional dependency X -> Y when **Y is functionally dependent on X** (where X is the **determinant set** and Y is the **dependent attribute**).

Let's illustrate a scenario where the designer didn't take in consideration dependencies between columns.

- Data (studID, studName, address, courseID, courseName, grade).

The following structure is considerably better:

- Student (studID, studName, address).
- Course (courseID, courseName).
- Enrolled (studID, courseID, grade).

How do we pass from one to the other? That's what **schema refinement** does through **functional dependencies**.

A unique way to represent a student is through his studID. Each student has his own address, hence we can say that studID determines *address*. We'll write this in the following way:

- studID - > address

In the previous example, we actually have the following FDs:

- studID - > studName, address
- courseID - > courseName
- studID, courseID - > grade

Let's have a look at the properties of functional dependencies in the case where X, Y and Z are attributes belonging to a table R:

- **Transitivity:** if we assume that X - > Y and Y - > Z, then it's clear that X - > Z.
- **Reflexivity:** if Y is a subset of X, then X -> Y.
- **Augmentation:** if X - > Y, then for any Z we'll have X, Z - > Y, Z.
- **Union:** if X - > Y and Y - > Z, then X - > Y, Z.
- **Decomposition:** if X -> Y, Z then X - > Y and X - > Z.

The first 3 properties are called the **Armstrong's Axioms**.

If F is a set of functional dependencies, F+ is the set of all FDs **logically implied** by F. **logically implied** is just another way of saying *obtained from the properties of functional dependencies* (the ones that we just enumerated). F+is also called **the closure of the set of functional dependencies**. Is the set of all dependencies logically implied by those present in F.

Let's illustrate the usage of those properties with an example. If we have the following set of FDs, can we conclude that A - > H is logically implied?

- A - > B
- A - > C
- C, G - > H
- C, G - > I
- B - > H

Let's see which properties are applicable to our case:

- We know that, by the transitivity property, if X -> Y and Y - > Z then we have X -> Z.
- In our case we have A - > B and B - > H.
- Hence, by transitivity, A - > H is logically implied.

Which other dependencies are parts of the closure?

- CG -> HI by the union rule.
- AG -> I by noticing that A -> C holds, and then AG -> CG by the augmentation rule and then AG -> I by transitivity.

Given a set of FDs, is there a faster way to compute if a dependency is logically implied?

Let's see through an example how we can ask this question in multiple ways:

- Does F = {A - > B, B - > C, C D - > E} imply A - > E?
- Is A - > E in the closure F+ ?
- Is E in A+?

Before going on with a linear time algorithm, we notice that we've introduced a new notion, A+. We call A+ the **attribute closure of A** with respect to F and it will help us figure out if A - > E is logically implied.

1. Assume that we create a **temporary attribute closure of A** called TMP and that to begin, TMP = A (the input of the FDs that you want to verify).
2. Let's consider the first given dependency of F, A - > B.
3. Is A in the **TMP**? Yes, since as stated previously TMP = A; we continue.
4. If we continue, we union B with the current TMP, A. What we obtain is the new TMP, AB (since A union B = AB).
5. We now consider the second given dependency, B - > C.
6. Is B in the **TMP**? Yes, since we now have AB in the TMP; we continue.
7. If we continue, we union C with the current TMP, AB. What we obtain is the new TMP, ABC (since AB union C = ABC).
8. We consider the 3rd given dependency, C D - > E.
9. Is CD in the **TMP**? No, since we only have ABC in the current TMP, hence we stop.
10. The **attribute closure of A** is then A+ = TMP = {A, B, C}.

Now, to check if A - > E is in the closure F+, we can conclude that since E is **NOT** in A+, then A - > E is **NOT** in F+.

We can generalize this into an algorithm:

1. Consider the input of your FDs as the first element of your **temporary attribute closure** TMP.
2. Consider each dependency X - > Y of the given set of FDs.
3. Is X part of **TMP**? If yes, continue to step 4. If no, continue to step 5.
4. Yes: Union TMP with Y.
5. No: Your attribute closure = TMP (your current temporary attribute closure from step 3).

Conclusion: if an attribute is in your attribute closure, then it's logically implied (its part of the closure of the set of functional dependencies).

Now that we know how to quickly verify if a dependency is **logically implied**... how do we find all the dependencies that are logically implied? Given a set of FDs F, how do we find its closure, F+ ?

Let's go through an example again:

Given F = {A - > B, B - > C}, compute F+

The algorithm is pretty simple:

1. Build an empty matrix with all possible combinations of attributes as rows and columns.

	A	B	C	AB	AC	BC	ABC
A							
B							
C							
AB							
AC							
BC							
ABC							

2. Compute the attribute closures of all attribute combinations.

	Attribute closure
A+	ABC
B+	BC
C+	C
(AB)+	ABC
(AC)+	ABC
(BC)+	BC
(ABC)+	ABC

3. Fill the matrix from step 1) by putting a check mark when a row member Y (from the table defined in step 1) is part of a member of the attribute closure Y+ (from the table defined in step 2).

	A	B	C	AB	AC	BC	ABC
A	X	X	X	X	X	X	X
B		X	X			X	
C			X				
AB	X	X	X	X	X	X	X
AC	X	X	X	X	X	X	X
BC		X	X			X	
ABC	X	X	X	X	X	X	X

Let's look at some examples.

- Row member A: A, B, C, AB, AC, BC and ABC are all attributes of the closure of A+, ABC.

- Row member BC. A is not a member of attribute closure (BC)+ : we don't put a check mark because there is no A in (BC)+. However, we check B and C and BC.

- Row member C. A is not a member of (C+): we don't check it because C+ contains only C.

By having a check-mark at say the intersection of row A with column BC we mean that A - > BC is part of the closure F+. This is how we enumerate all the dependencies that are part of the closure F+.

Functional dependencies can also be used to find all the **candidate keys**. By definition, a candidate key is *a set of columns that can be uniquely used to identify a database record without any irrelevant/unrelated/superfluous data*. It is a reduction of the entire collection of attributes, hence a minimization.

Since we are talking about a minimal subset, we can start with the complete set of attributes and then, following functional dependencies, minimize the set until we reach the candidate keys (a set of attributes that cannot be reduced). Let's illustrate this once more by an example.

Say we have F = {A - > B, BC - > E and ED - > A}.

1. We know that the set of all attributes is ABCDE.
2. Can we reduce the set by using the first given FD? If we follow A - > B, we can remove B from the main set because B depends on A, and ABCD already contains A, hence no need of any dependent superfluous attribute. We obtain ACDE.
3. Can we reduce the set by using the second FD? If we follow BC - > E, we can remove E from the main set because E depends on BC, and ABCDE already contains BC. We obtain ABCD.
4. Can we reduce the set by using the third FD? If we follow ED - > A, we can remove A from the main set because A depends on ED, and ABCDE already contains ED. We obtain BCDE.
5. We now have a new set of attributes: ACDE, ABCD and BCDE. Let's call them X.
6. Can we simplify any attribute from X by using dependency A - > B ? We can remove B from ABCD because ABCD already contains A, and B depends on A: we obtain ACD. Can we do the same for BCDE? No, because BCDE doesn't contain A.

7. Can we simplify any attribute from X by using BC - > E ? We can remove E from BCDE because BCDE already contains BC and E depends on BC: we obtain BCD. Can we do the same for ACDE? No, because ACDE doesn't contain BC.

8. Can we simplify any attribute from X by using ED - > A? We can remove A from ACDE because ACDE already contains CD and A depends on CD: we obtain CDE.

9. We now have a new set of attributes: ACD, BCD and CDE. Let's call them Y.

10. Can we simplify any attribute from Y by using A - > B? BCD cannot be simplified because it doesn't contain A, and the rest of attributes from Y don't contain B.

11. Can we simplify any attribute from Y by using BC - > E? CDE cannot be simplified because it doesn't contain BC, and the rest of attributes from Y don't contain E.

12. Can we simplify any attribute from Y by using ED - > A? ACD cannot be simplified because it doesn't contain ED, and the rest of attributes from Y don't contain ED.

Conclusion: the functional dependencies from F cannot be used to simplify the subsets from Y, hence they cannot be more minimized. They are our candidate keys: ACD, BCD and CDE.

We notice that functional dependencies help us structuring our tables around unique attributes, avoiding superfluous information.

3.3.   Other Kinds of Dependencies

Multivalued Dependency

- Multivalued dependency occurs when two attributes in a table are independent of each other but, both depend on a third attribute.

- A multivalued dependency consists of at least two attributes that are dependent on a third attribute that's why it always requires at least three attributes.

Example: Suppose there is a bike manufacturer company which produces two colors (white and black) of each model every year.

BIKE_MODEL	MANUF_YEAR	COLOR
M2011	2008	White
M2001	2008	Black
M3001	2013	White
M3001	2013	Black
M4006	2017	White
M4006	2017	Black

Here columns COLOR and MANUF_YEAR are dependent on BIKE_MODEL and independent of each other.

In this case, these two columns can be called as multivalued dependent on BIKE_MODEL. The representation of these dependencies is shown below:

- BIKE_MODEL $\rightarrow \rightarrow$ MANUF_YEAR
- BIKE_MODEL $\rightarrow \rightarrow$ COLOR

This can be read as "BIKE_MODEL multidetermined MANUF_YEAR" and "BIKE_MODEL multidetermined COLOR".

Join Dependency

- Join decomposition is a further generalization of multivalued dependencies.
- If the join of R1 and R2 over C is equal to relation R, then we can say that a join dependency (JD) exists.
- Where R1 and R2 are the decompositions R1 (A, B, C) and R2(C, D) of a given relations R (A, B, C, D).
- Alternatively, R1 and R2 are a lossless decomposition of R.
- A JD $\bowtie$ {R1, R2,..., Rn} is said to hold over a relation R if R1, R2,....., Rn is a lossless-join decomposition.
- The *(A, B, C, D), (C, D) will be a JD of R if the join of join's attribute is equal to the relation R.
- Here, *(R1, R2, R3) is used to indicate that relation R1, R2, R3 and so on are a JD of R.

Inclusion Dependency

- Multivalued dependency and join dependency can be used to guide database design although they both are less common than functional dependencies.
- Inclusion dependencies are quite common. They typically show little influence on designing of the database.
- The inclusion dependency is a statement in which some columns of a relation are contained in other columns.
- The example of inclusion dependency is a foreign key. In one relation, the referring relation is contained in the primary key column(s) of the referenced relation.

- Suppose we have two relations R and S which was obtained by translating two entity sets such that every R entity is also an S entity.

- Inclusion dependency would be happen if projecting R on its key attributes yields a relation that is contained in the relation obtained by projecting S on its key attributes.

- In inclusion dependency, we should not split groups of attributes that participate in an inclusion dependency.

- In practice, most inclusion dependencies are key-based that is involved only keys.

CHAPTER 4

4. Transaction Management

4.1.   Transaction

- The transaction is a set of logically related operation. It contains a group of tasks.

- A transaction is an action or series of actions. It is performed by a single user to perform operations for accessing the contents of the database.

Example: Suppose an employee of bank transfers Rs 800 from X's account to Y's account. This small transaction contains several low-level tasks:

X's Account

    Open_Account(X)
    Old_Balance = X.balance
    New_Balance = Old_Balance - 800
    X.balance = New_Balance
    Close_Account(X)

Y's Account

    Open_Account(Y)
    Old_Balance = Y.balance
    New_Balance = Old_Balance + 800
    Y.balance = New_Balance
    Close_Account(Y)

Operations of Transaction

Following are the main operations of transaction:

- **Read(X):** Read operation is used to read the value of X from the database and stores it in a buffer in main memory.

- **Write(X):** Write operation is used to write the value back to the database from the buffer.

Let's take an example to debit transaction from an account which consists of following operations:

    1. R(X);
    2. X = X - 500;
    3. W(X);

Let's assume the value of X before starting of the transaction is 4000.

- The first operation reads X's value from database and stores it in a buffer.
- The second operation will decrease the value of X by 500. So buffer will contain 3500.
- The third operation will write the buffer's value to the database. So X's final value will be 3500.

But it may be possible that because of the failure of hardware, software or power, etc. that transaction may fail before finished all the operations in the set.

For example: If in the above transaction, the debit transaction fails after executing operation 2 then X's value will remain 4000 in the database which is not acceptable by the bank.

To solve this problem, we have two important operations:

- **Commit:** It is used to save the work done permanently.
- **Rollback:** It is used to undo the work done.

The transaction has the four properties. These are used to maintain consistency in a database, before and after the transaction.

Property of Transaction

- Atomicity
- Consistency
- Isolation
- Durability

Atomicity

- It states that all operations of the transaction take place at once if not, the transaction is aborted.
- There is no midway, i.e., the transaction cannot occur partially. Each transaction is treated as one unit and either run to completion or is not executed at all.

Atomicity involves the following two operations:

- **Abort:** If a transaction aborts then all the changes made are not visible.
- **Commit:** If a transaction commits then all the changes made are visible.

Example: Let's assume that following transaction T consisting of T1 and T2. A consists of Rs 600 and B consists of Rs 300. Transfer Rs 100 from account A to account B.

T1	T2
Read(A) A:= A-100 Write(A)	Read(B) Y:= Y+100 Write(B)

After completion of the transaction, A consists of Rs 500 and B consists of Rs 400.

If the transaction T fails after the completion of transaction T1 but before completion of transaction T2, then the amount will be deducted from A but not added to B. This shows the inconsistent database state. In order to ensure correctness of database state, the transaction must be executed in entirety.

Consistency

- The integrity constraints are maintained so that the database is consistent before and after the transaction.

- The execution of a transaction will leave a database in either its prior stable state or a new stable state.

- The consistent property of database states that every transaction sees a consistent database instance.

- The transaction is used to transform the database from one consistent state to another consistent state.

For example: The total amount must be maintained before or after the transaction.

- Total before T occurs = 600+300=900

- Total after T occurs= 500+400=900

Therefore, the database is consistent. In the case when T1 is completed but T2 fails, then inconsistency will occur.

Isolation

- It shows that the data which is used at the time of execution of a transaction cannot be used by the second transaction until the first one is completed.

- In isolation, if the transaction T1 is being executed and using the data item X, then that data item can't be accessed by any other transaction T2 until the transaction T1 ends.

- The concurrency control subsystem of the DBMS enforced the isolation property.

Durability

- The durability property is used to indicate the performance of the database's consistent state. It states that the transaction made the permanent changes.

- They cannot be lost by the erroneous operation of a faulty transaction or by the system failure. When a transaction is completed, then the database reaches a state known as the consistent state. That consistent state cannot be lost, even in the event of a system's failure.

- The recovery subsystem of the DBMS has the responsibility of Durability property.

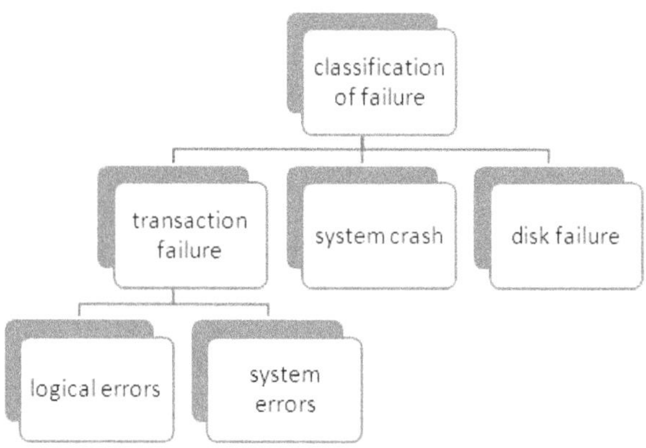

Classification of Failure

To see wherever the matter has occurred, we tend to generalize a failure into numerous classes, as follows:

- Transaction failure
- System crash
- Disk failure

Transaction failure: A transaction needs to abort once it fails to execute or once it reaches to any further extent from wherever it can't go to any extent further. This is often known as transaction failure wherever solely many transactions or processes are hurt. The reasons for transaction failure are:

- Logical errors
- System errors

Logical errors: Where a transaction cannot complete as a result of its code error or an internal error condition.

System errors: Wherever the information system itself terminates an energetic transaction as a result of the DBMS isn't able to execute it, or it's to prevent due to some system condition. to Illustrate, just in case of situation or resource inconvenience, the system aborts an active transaction.

System crash: There are issues – external to the system – that will cause the system to prevent abruptly and cause the system to crash. For instance, interruptions in power supply might cause the failure of underlying hardware or software package failure. Examples might include OS errors.

Disk failure: In early days of technology evolution, it had been a typical drawback wherever hard-disk drives or storage drives accustomed to failing oftentimes. Disk failures include the formation of dangerous sectors, unreachability to the disk, disk crash or the other failure, that destroys all or a section of disk storage.

4.2. Storage Structure

Classification of storage structure is as explained below:

- **Volatile storage:** As the name suggests, a memory board (volatile storage) cannot survive system crashes. Volatile storage devices are placed terribly near to the CPU; usually, they're embedded on the chipset itself. For instance, main memory and cache memory are samples of the memory board. They're quick however will store a solely little quantity of knowledge.

- **Non-volatile storage:** These recollections are created to survive system crashes. they're immense in information storage capability, however slower in the accessibility. Examples could include hard-disks, magnetic tapes, flash memory, and non-volatile (battery backed up) RAM.

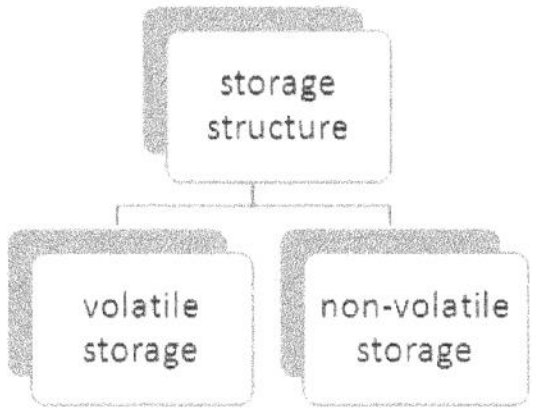

Recovery and Atomicity

When a system crashes, it should have many transactions being executed and numerous files opened for them to switch the information items. Transactions are a product of numerous operations that are atomic in nature. However consistent with ACID properties of a database, atomicity of transactions as an entire should be maintained, that is, either all the operations are executed or none.

When a database management system recovers from a crash, it ought to maintain the subsequent:

- It ought to check the states of all the transactions that were being executed.

- A transaction could also be within the middle of some operation; the database management system should make sure the atomicity of the transaction during this case.

- It ought to check whether or not the transaction is completed currently or it must be rolled back.

- No transactions would be allowed to go away from the database management system in an inconsistent state.

There are 2 forms of techniques, which may facilitate a database management system in recovering as well as maintaining the atomicity of a transaction:

- Maintaining the logs of every transaction, and writing them onto some stable storage before truly modifying the info.

- Maintaining shadow paging, wherever the changes are done on a volatile memory, and later, and the particular info is updated.

Log-based Recovery or Manual Recovery

Log could be a sequence of records, which maintains the records of actions performed by dealing. It's necessary that the logs area unit written before the particular modification and hold on a stable storage media, that is failsafe. Log-based recovery works as follows:

- The log file is unbroken on a stable storage media.

- When a transaction enters the system and starts execution, it writes a log regarding it.

Recovery with Concurrent Transactions (Automated Recovery)

When over one transaction is being executed in parallel, the logs are interleaved. At the time of recovery, it'd become exhausting for the recovery system to go back all logs, and so begin recovering. To ease this example, the latest package uses the idea of 'checkpoints'. Automated Recovery is of three types.

- Deferred Update Recovery

- Immediate Update Recovery

- Shadow Paging

States of Transaction

In a database, the transaction can be in one of the following states:

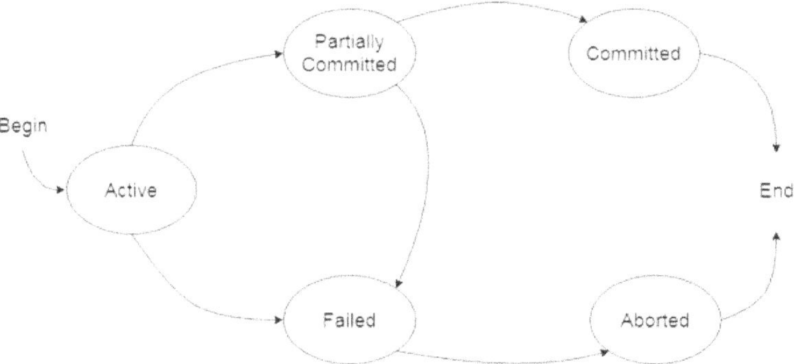

Active State

- The active state is the first state of every transaction. In this state, the transaction is being executed.

- For example: Insertion or deletion or updating a record is done here. But all the records are still not saved to the database.

Partially Committed

- In the partially committed state, a transaction executes its final operation, but the data is still not saved to the database.

- In the total mark calculation example, a final display of the total marks step is executed in this state.

Committed

A transaction is said to be in a committed state if it executes all its operations successfully. In this state, all the effects are now permanently saved on the database system.

Failed State

- If any of the checks made by the database recovery system fails, then the transaction is said to be in the failed state.

- In the example of total mark calculation, if the database is not able to fire a query to fetch the marks, then the transaction will fail to execute.

Aborted

- If any of the checks fail and the transaction has reached a failed state then the database recovery system will make sure that the database is in its previous consistent state. If not then it will abort or roll back the transaction to bring the database into a consistent state.

- If the transaction fails in the middle of the transaction then before executing the transaction, all the executed transactions are rolled back to its consistent state.

- After aborting the transaction, the database recovery module will select one of the two operations:
  - Re-start the transaction
  - Kill the transaction

Transaction Isolation

Isolation levels determine the type of phenomena that can occur during the execution of concurrent transactions.

eDeveloper sets this property only for the following databases: MSSQL, Informix and DB2.

Three phenomena define SQL Isolation levels for a transaction:

- **Dirty Reads** returns different results within a single transaction when an SQL operation an uncommitted or modified record created by another transaction. Dirty Reads increases concurrency, but reduces consistency.

- **Non-Repeatable Reads** returns different results within a single transaction when an SQL operation reads the same row in a table twice. Non-Repeatable Reads can occur when another transaction modifies and commits a change to the row between transaction reads. Non-repeatable reads increases consistency, but reduces concurrency.

- **Phantoms** return different results within a single transaction when an SQL operation retrieves a range of data values twice. Phantoms can occur if another transaction inserted a new record and committed the insertion between executions of the range retrieval. Each Isolation level differs in the phenomena it allows:

Isolation Level	Dirty Reads	Read Committed	Repeatable Read	Can be Serialized
Dirty Read Allowed	Yes	No	No	No
Non-Repeatable Read Allowed	Yes	Yes	No	No
Phantoms Allowed	Yes	Yes	Yes	No

- **Read Committed:** Specifies that shared locks are held while the data is being read to avoid dirty reads, but the data can be changed before the end of the transaction, resulting in non-repeatable reads or phantom data. This option is the SQL Server default.

- **Can be Serialized:** Places a range lock on the data set, preventing other users from updating or inserting rows into the data set until the transaction is complete. This is the most restrictive of the four Isolation levels. Because concurrency is lower, use this option only when necessary. This option has the same effect as setting HOLDLOCK on all tables in all SELECT statements in a transaction.

Serializability

- Serializability is a concurrency scheme where the concurrent transaction is equivalent to one that executes the transactions serially.

- A schedule is a list of transactions.

- Serial schedule defines each transaction is executed consecutively without any interference from other transactions.

- Non-serial schedule defines the operations from a group of concurrent transactions that are interleaved.

- In non-serial schedule, if the schedule is not proper, then the problems can arise like multiple update, uncommitted dependency and incorrect analysis.

- The main objective of serializability is to find non-serial schedules that allow transactions to execute concurrently without interference and produce a database state that could be produced by a serial execution.

1. Conflict Serializability

- Conflict serializability defines two instructions of two different transactions accessing the same data item to perform a read/write operation.

- It deals with detecting the instructions that are conflicting in any way and specifying the order in which the instructions should execute in case there is any conflict.

- A conflict serializability arises when one of the instructions is a write operation.

The Following Rules are Important in Conflict Serializability

- If two transactions are both read operation, then they are not in conflict.

- If one transaction wants to perform a read operation and other transaction wants to perform a write operation, then they are in conflict and cannot be swapped.

- If both the transactions are for write operation, then they are in conflict, but can be allowed to take place in any order, because the transactions do not read the value updated by each other.

2. View Serializability

- View serializability is another type of serializability.

- It can be derived by creating another schedule out of an existing schedule and involves the same set of transactions.

Example: Let us assume two transactions T1 and T2 that are being serialized to create two different schedules SH1 and SH2, where T1 and T2 want to access the same data item.

Now there can be three scenarios:

- **If in SH1, T1** reads the initial value of data item, and then in SH2, T1 should read the initial value of that same data item.

- **If in SH2, T1** writes a value in the data item which is read by T2, and then in SH2, T1 should write the value in the data item before T2 reads it.

- **If in SH1, T1** performs the final write operation on that data item, and then in SH2, T1 should perform the final write operation on that data item.

- If a concurrent schedule is view equivalent to a serial schedule of same transaction then it is said to be **View serializable.**

A series of operation from one transaction to another transaction is known as schedule. It is used to preserve the order of the operation in each of the individual transaction.

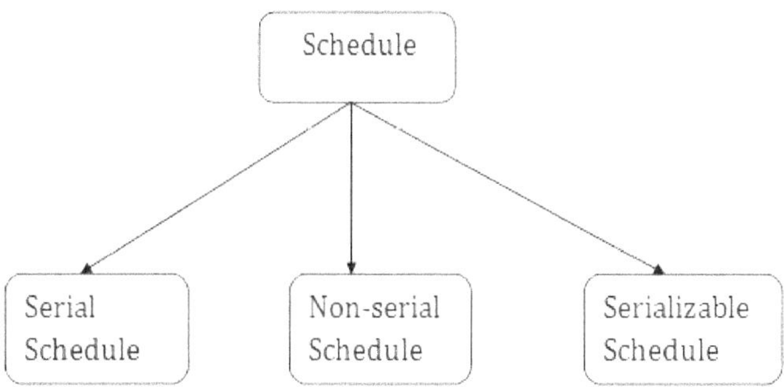

1. Serial Schedule

The serial schedule is a type of schedule where one transaction is executed completely before starting another transaction. In the serial schedule, when the first transaction completes its cycle, then the next transaction is executed.

For example: Suppose there are two transactions T1 and T2 which have some operations. If it has no interleaving of operations, then there are the following two possible outcomes:

- Execute all the operations of T1 which was followed by all the operations of T2.
- Execute all the operations of T1 which was followed by all the operations of T2.
    - In the given (a) figure, Schedule A shows the serial schedule where T1 followed by T2.
    - In the given (b) figure, Schedule B shows the serial schedule where T2 followed by T1.

2. Non-serial Schedule

- If interleaving of operations is allowed, then there will be non-serial schedule.
- It contains many possible orders in which the system can execute the individual operations of the transactions.
- In the given figure (c) and (d), Schedule C and Schedule D are the non-serial schedules. It has interleaving of operations.

3. Serializable Schedule

- The serializability of schedules is used to find non-serial schedules that allow the transaction to execute concurrently without interfering with one another.

- It identifies which schedules are correct when executions of the transaction have interleaving of their operations.

- A non-serial schedule will be serializable if its result is equal to the result of its transactions executed serially.

(a)

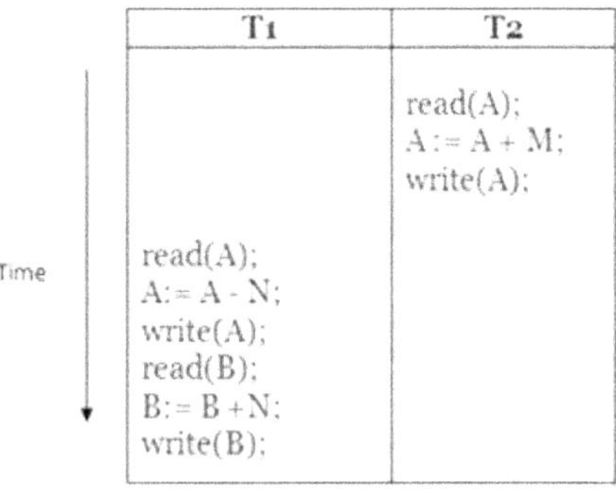

T1	T2

read(A);
A := A – N;
write(A);
read(B);
B := B + N;
write(B);	

	read(A);
	A := A + M;
	write(A);

Schedule A

(b)

T1	T2

	read(A);
	A := A + M;
	write(A);

read(A);
A := A - N;
write(A);
read(B);
B := B + N;
write(B);	

Schedule B

(c)

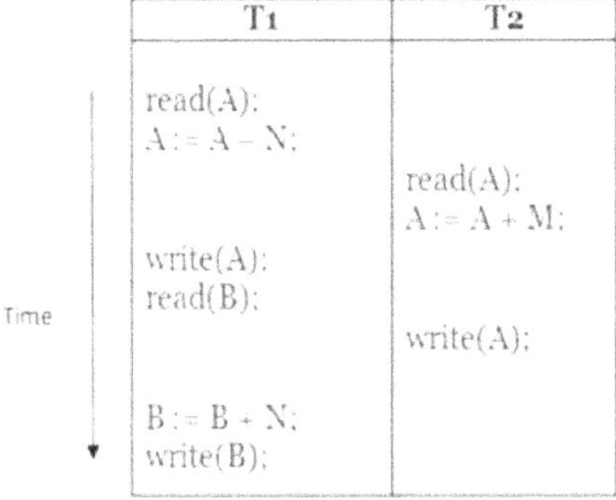

Schedule C

(d)

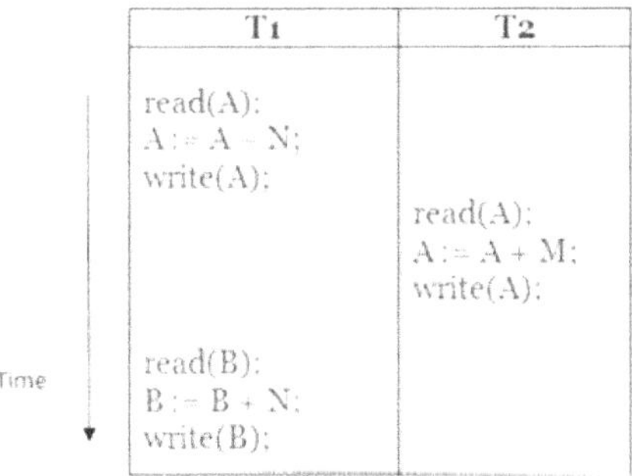

Schedule D

Schedule A and Schedule B are serial schedule.

Schedule C and Schedule D are Non-serial schedule.

4.3.   Transaction Isolation and Atomicity Transaction Isolation Levels

Transaction isolation levels are a measure of the extent to which transaction isolation succeeds. In particular, transaction isolation levels are defined by the presence or absence of the following phenomena:

- **Dirty Reads** A *dirty read* occurs when a transaction reads data that has not yet been committed. For example, suppose transaction 1 updates a row. Transaction 2 reads the updated row before transaction 1 commits the update. If transaction 1 rolls back the change, transaction 2 will have read data that is considered never to have existed.

- **Nonrepeatable Reads** A *nonrepeatable read* occurs when a transaction reads the same row twice but gets different data each time. For example, suppose transaction 1 reads a row. Transaction 2 updates or deletes that row and commits the update or delete. If transaction 1 rereads the row, it retrieves different row values or discovers that the row has been deleted.

- **Phantoms** A *phantom* is a row that matches the search criteria but is not initially seen. For example, suppose transaction 1 reads a set of rows that satisfy some search criteria. Transaction 2 generates a new row (through either an update or an insert) that matches the search criteria for transaction 1. If transaction 1 reexecutes the statement that reads the rows, it gets a different set of rows.

The four transaction isolation levels (as defined by SQL-92) are defined in terms of these phenomena. In the following table, an "X" marks each phenomenon that can occur.

Transaction isolation level	Dirty reads	Nonrepeatable reads	Phantoms
Read uncommitted	X	X	X
Read committed	--	X	X
Repeatable read	--	--	X
Serializable	--	--	--

The following table describes simple ways that a DBMS might implement the transaction isolation levels.

Important

Most DBMSs use more complex schemes than these to increase concurrency. These examples are provided for illustration purposes only. In particular, ODBC does not prescribe how particular DBMSs isolate transactions from each other.

Transaction isolation	Possible implementation
Read uncommitted	Transactions are not isolated from each other. If the DBMS supports other transaction isolation levels, it ignores whatever mechanism it uses to implement those levels. So that they do not adversely affect other transactions, transactions running at the Read Uncommitted level are usually read-only.
Read committed	The transaction waits until rows write-locked by other transactions are unlocked; this prevents it from reading any "dirty" data. The transaction holds a read lock (if it only reads the row) or write lock (if it updates or deletes the row) on the current row to prevent other transactions from updating or deleting it. The transaction releases read locks when it moves off the current row. It holds write locks until it is committed or rolled back.
Repeatable read	The transaction waits until rows write-locked by other transactions are unlocked; this prevents it from reading any "dirty" data. The transaction holds read locks on all rows it returns to the application and write locks on all rows it inserts, updates, or deletes. For example, if the transaction includes the SQL statement SELECT * FROM Orders, the transaction read-locks rows as the application fetches them. If the transaction includes the SQL statement DELETE FROM Orders WHERE Status = 'CLOSED', the transaction write-locks rows as it deletes them. Because other transactions cannot update or delete these rows, the current transaction avoids any nonrepeatable reads. The transaction releases its locks when it is committed or rolled back.
Serializable	The transaction waits until rows write-locked by other transactions are unlocked; this prevents it from reading any "dirty" data. The transaction holds a read lock (if it only reads rows) or write lock (if it can update or delete rows) on the range of rows it affects. For example, if the transaction includes the SQL statement SELECT * FROM Orders, the range is the entire Orders table; the transaction read-locks the table and does not allow any new rows to be inserted into it. If the transaction includes the SQL statement DELETE FROM Orders WHERE Status = 'CLOSED', the range is all rows with a Status of "CLOSED"; the transaction write-locks all rows in the Orders table with a Status of "CLOSED" and does not allow any rows to be inserted or updated such that the resulting row has a Status of "CLOSED". Because other transactions cannot update or delete the rows in the range, the current transaction avoids any nonrepeatable reads. Because other transactions cannot insert any rows in the range, the current transaction avoids any phantoms. The transaction releases its lock when it is committed or rolled back.

Concurrency Control

- Concurrency control manages the transactions simultaneously without letting them interfere with each another.

- The main objective of concurrency control is to allow many users perform different operations at the same time.

- Using more than one transaction concurrently improves the performance of system.

- If we are not able to perform the operations concurrently, then there can be serious problems such as loss of data integrity and consistency.

- Concurrency control increases the throughput because of handling multiple transactions simultaneously.

- It reduces waiting time of transaction.

Example

- Consider two transactions T1 and T2.
  - **T1:** Deposits Rs. 1000 to both accounts X and Y.
  - **T2:** Doubles the balance of accounts X and Y.

    T1

    Read (X)

    $X \leftarrow X + 1000$

    Write (X)

    Read (Y)

    $Y \leftarrow Y + 1000$

    Write (Y)

    T2

    Read (X)

    $X \leftarrow X * 2$

    Write (X)

    Read (Y)

    $Y \leftarrow Y * 2$

    Write (Y)

The above two transactions can be executed concurrently as below:

Schedule C1

T1	T2	X	Y	Operations
		1000	1000	
Read (X)		1000		
X ← X + 1000		1000 + 1000		
Write (X)		2000		
	Read (X)	2000		
	X ← X * 2	2000 * 2		
	Write (X)	4000		
Read (Y)				
Y ← Y + 1000				
Write (Y)			2000	
	Read (Y)			
	Y ← Y * 2			
	Write (Y)		4000	
		4000	4000	Final Balance

The above concurrent schedule executes in the following manner:

- Step 1: Part of transaction (T1) is executed, which updates X to Rs. 2000.
- Step 2: The processor switches to transaction (T2). T2 is executed and updates X to Rs. 4000. Then the processor switches to transaction (T1) and remaining part of T2 which updates Y to Rs. 2000 is executed.
- Step 3: At the end of remaining part of T2 which reads Y as Rs. 2000, updates it to Rs. 4000 by multiplying value of Y.

This concurrent schedule maintains the consistency of database as,

$$X + Y = 2000 + 2000 = 4000$$

Remains unchanged.

Therefore, the above schedule can be converted to equivalent serial schedule and hence it is a consistent schedule.

Concurrency control can be divided into two protocols:

- Lock-Based Protocol
- Timestamp Based Protocol

1. Lock-Based Protocol

- Lock is a mechanism which is important in a concurrent control.
- It controls concurrent access to a data item.
- It assures that one process should not retrieve or update a record which another process is updating.

For example, in traffic, there are signals which indicate stop and go. When one signal is allowed to pass at a time, then other signals are locked. Similarly, in database transaction only one transaction is performed at a time and other transactions are locked.

- If the locking is not done properly, then it will display the inconsistent and corrupt data.
- It manages the order between the conflicting pairs among transactions at the time of execution.

There are Two Lock Modes

- Shared Lock
- Exclusive Lock

Shared Locks are represented by S. The data items can only read without performing modification to it from the database. S – lock is requested using lock – s instruction.

Exclusive Locks are represented by X. The data items can be read as well as written. X – lock is requested using lock – X instruction.

Lock Compatibility Matrix

Lock Compatibility Matrix controls whether multiple transactions can acquire locks on the same resource at the same time.

	Shared	*Exclusive*
Shared	True	False
Exclusive	False	False

- If a resource is already locked by another transaction, then a new lock request can be granted only if the mode of the requested lock is compatible with the mode of the existing lock.

- Any number of transactions can hold shared locks on an item, but if any transaction holds an exclusive lock on item, no other transaction may hold any lock on the item.

2. Timestamp based Protocol

- Timestamp Based Protocol helps DBMS to identify the transactions.

- It is a unique identifier. Each transaction is issued a timestamp when it enters into the system.

- Timestamp protocol determines the serializability order.

- It is most commonly used concurrency protocol.

- It uses either system time or logical counter as a timestamp.

- It starts working as soon as a transaction is created.

Timestamp Ordering Protocol

- The TO Protocol ensures serializability among transactions in their conflicting read and write operations.

- The transaction of timestamp (T) is denoted as TS(T).

- Data item (X) of read timestamp is denoted by R–timestamp(X).

- Data item (X) of write timestamp is denoted by W–timestamp(X).

Following are the Timestamp Ordering Algorithms

1. Basic Timestamp Ordering

- It compares the timestamp of T with Read_TS(X) and Write_TS(X) to ensure that the transaction execution is not violated.

- If the transaction execution order is violated, transaction T is aborted and resubmitted to the system as a new transaction with a new timestamp.

2. Strict Timestamp Ordering

- It ensures that the schedules are both strict for easy recoverability and conflict serializability.

3. Thomas's Write Rule

It does not enforce conflict serializability. It rejects some write operations, by modifying the checks for the write_item(X) operation as follows:

- If Read_TS(X) > TS(T) (read timestamp is greater than timestamp transaction), then abort and rollback transaction T and reject the operation.
- If Write_TS(X) > TS(T) (write timestamp is greater than timestamp transaction), then do not execute the write operation but continue processing. Because some transaction with a timestamp is greater than TS(T) and after T in the timestamp has already written the value of X.
- If neither the condition transaction 1 nor the condition in transaction 2 occurs, then execute the Write_item(X) operation of transaction T and set Write_TS(X) to TS(T).

Multiple Granularity

Let's start by understanding the meaning of granularity.

Granularity: It is the size of data item allowed to lock.

Multiple Granularity

- It can be defined as hierarchically breaking up the database into blocks which can be locked.
- The Multiple Granularity protocol enhances concurrency and reduces lock overhead.
  - It maintains the track of what to lock and how to lock.
  - It makes easy to decide either to lock a data item or to unlock a data item. This type of hierarchy can be graphically represented as a tree.

For example: Consider a tree which has four levels of nodes.

- The first level or higher level shows the entire database.
- The second level represents a node of type area. The higher level database consists of exactly these areas.
- The area consists of children nodes which are known as files. No file can be present in more than one area.
- Finally, each file contains child nodes known as records. The file has exactly those records that are its child nodes. No records represent in more than one file.

- Hence, the levels of the tree starting from the top level are as follows:
    - Database
    - Area
    - File
    - Record

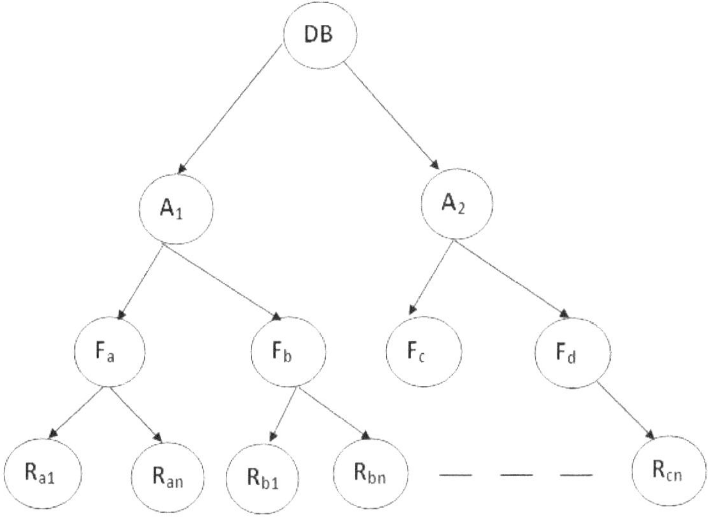

In this example, the highest level shows the entire database. The levels below are file, record, and fields.

There are three additional lock modes with multiple granularities:

Intention Mode Lock

- **Intention-shared (IS):** It contains explicit locking at a lower level of the tree but only with shared locks.
- **Intention-Exclusive (IX):** It contains explicit locking at a lower level with exclusive or shared locks.
- **Shared & Intention-Exclusive (SIX):** In this lock, the node is locked in shared mode, and some node is locked in exclusive mode by the same transaction.
- **Compatibility Matrix with Intention Lock Modes:** The below table describes the compatibility matrix for these lock modes:

	IS	IX	S	SIX	X
IS	✓	✓	✓	✓	✗
IX	✓	✓	✗	✗	✗
S	✓	✗	✓	✗	✗
SIX	✓	✗	✗	✗	✗
X	✗	✗	✗	✗	✗

It uses the intention lock modes to ensure serializability. It requires that if a transaction attempts to lock a node, then that node must follow these protocols:

- Transaction T1 should follow the lock-compatibility matrix.

- Transaction T1 firstly locks the root of the tree. It can lock it in any mode.

- If T1 currently has the parent of the node locked in either IX or IS mode, then the transaction T1 will lock a node in S or IS mode only.

- If T1 currently has the parent of the node locked in either IX or SIX modes, then the transaction T1 will lock a node in X, SIX, or IX mode only.

- If T1 has not previously unlocked any node only, then the Transaction T1 can lock a node.

- If T1 currently has none of the children of the node-locked only, then Transaction T1 will unlock a node.

Observe that in multiple-granularity, the locks are acquired in top-down order, and locks must be released in bottom-up order.

- If transaction T1 reads record R_{a9} in file F_a, then transaction T1 needs to lock the database, area A_1 and file F_a in IX mode. Finally, it needs to lock R_{a2} in S mode.

- If transaction T2 modifies record R_{a9} in file F_a, then it can do so after locking the database, area A_1 and file F_a in IX mode. Finally, it needs to lock the R_{a9} in X mode.

- If transaction T3 reads all the records in file F_a, then transaction T3 needs to lock the database and area A in IS mode. At last, it needs to lock F_a in S mode.

- If transaction T4 reads the entire database, then T4 needs to lock the database in S mode.

Validation-Based Protocols

Validation phase is also known as optimistic concurrency control technique. In the validation based protocol, the transaction is executed in the following three phases:

- **Read phase:** In this phase, the transaction T is read and executed. It is used to read the value of various data items and stores them in temporary local variables. It can perform all the write operations on temporary variables without an update to the actual database.

- **Validation phase:** In this phase, the temporary variable value will be validated against the actual data to see if it violates the serializability.

- **Write phase:** If the validation of the transaction is validated, then the temporary results are written to the database or system otherwise the transaction is rolled back.

Here each phase has the following different timestamps:

- **Start (Ti):** It contains the time when Ti started its execution.

- **Validation (Ti):** It contains the time when Ti finishes its read phase and starts its validation phase.

- **Finish (Ti):** It contains the time when Ti finishes its write phase.

This protocol is used to determine the time stamp for the transaction for serialization using the time stamp of the validation phase, as it is the actual phase which determines if the transaction will commit or rollback.

Hence TS (T) = validation (T).

The serializability is determined during the validation process. It can't be decided in advance.

While executing the transaction, it ensures a greater degree of concurrency and also less number of conflicts.

Thus it contains transactions which have less number of rollbacks.

Multiversion Concurrency Control Techniques

Multiversion concurrency control techniques keep the old values of a data item when the item is updated. Several versions (values) of an item are maintained. When a transaction requires access to an item, an appropriate version is chosen to maintain the serialisability of the concurrently executing schedule, if possible. The idea is that some read operations that would be rejected in other techniques can still be accepted, by reading an older version of the item to maintain serialisability.

An obvious drawback of multiversion techniques is that more storage is needed to maintain multiple versions of the database items. However, older versions may have to be maintained anyway – for example, for recovery purpose. In addition, some database applications require older versions to be kept to maintain a history of the evolution of data item values. The extreme case is a temporal database, which keeps track of all changes and the items at which they occurred. In such cases, there is no additional penalty for multiversion techniques, since older versions are already maintained.

Multiversion Techniques based on Timestamp Ordering

In this technique, several versions X1, X2, ... Xk of each data item X are kept by the system. For each version, the value of version Xi and the following two timestamps are kept:

- **read_TS(Xi):** The read timestamp of Xi; this is the largest of all the timestamps of transactions that have successfully read version Xi.

- **write_TS(Xi):** The write timestamp of Xi; this is the timestamp of the transaction that wrote the value of version Xi.

Whenever a transaction T is allowed to execute a write_item(X) operation, a new version of item X, Xk+1, is created, with both the write_TS(Xk+1) and the read_TS(Xk+1) set to TS(T). Correspondingly, when a transaction T is allowed to read the value of version Xi, the value of read_TS(Xi) is set to the largest of read_TS(Xi) and TS(T).

To ensure serialisability, we use the following two rules to control the reading and writing of data items:

- If transaction T issues a write_item(X) operation, and version i of X has the highest write_TS (Xi) of all versions of X which is also less than or equal to TS (T), and TS (T) < read_TS (Xi), then abort and roll back transaction T; otherwise, create a new version Xj of X with read_TS (Xj) = write_TS (Xj) = TS (T).

- If transaction T issues a read_item(X) operation, and version i of X has the highest write_TS (Xi) of all versions of X which is also less than or equal to TS (T), then return the value of Xi to transaction T, and set the value of read_TS(Xj) to the largest of TS(T) and the current read_TS(Xj).

Multiversion Two-Phase Locking

In this scheme, there are three locking modes for an item: read, write and certify. Hence, the state of an item X can be one of 'read locked', 'write locked', 'certify locked' and 'unlocked'. The idea behind the multiversion two-phase locking is to allow other transactions T' to read an item X while a single transaction T holds a write lock X. (Compare with standard locking scheme.) This is accomplished by allowing two versions for each item X; one version must always have been written by some committed transaction. The second version X' is created when a transaction T acquires a write lock on the item. Other transactions can continue to read the committed version X while T holds the write lock. Now transaction T can change the value of X' as needed, without affecting the value of the committed version X. However, once T is ready to commit, it must obtain a certify lock on all items that it currently holds write locks on before it can commit. The certify lock is not compatible with read locks, so the transaction may have to delay its commit until all its write lock items are released by any reading transactions. At this point, the committed version X of the data item is set to the value of version X', version X' is discarded, and the certify locks are then released. The lock compatibility table for this scheme is shown below:

	Read	Write	Certify
Read	Yes	Yes	No
Write	Yes	No	No
Certify	No	No	No

In this multiversion two-phase locking scheme, reads can proceed concurrently with a write operation – an arrangement not permitted under the standard two-phase locking schemes. The cost is that a transaction may have to delay its commit until it obtains exclusive certify locks on all items it has updated. It can be shown that this scheme avoids cascading aborts, since transactions are only allowed to read the version X that was written by committed transaction. However, deadlock may occur.

4.4. Database Backup

Database Backup is storage of data that means the copy of the data.

* It is a safeguard against unexpected data loss and application errors.
* It protects the database against data loss.
* If the original data is lost, then using the backup it can reconstruct.

The backups are divided into two types:

- Physical Backup
- Logical Backup

Physical Backups

- Physical Backups are the backups of the physical files used in storing and recovering your database, such as data files, control files and archived redo logs, log files.
- It is a copy of files storing database information to some other location, such as disk, some offline storage like magnetic tape.
- Physical backups are the foundation of the recovery mechanism in the database.
- Physical backup provides the minute details about the transaction and modification to the database.

Logical Backup

- Logical Backup contains logical data which is extracted from a database.
- It includes backup of logical data like views, procedures, functions, tables, etc.
- It is a useful supplement to physical backups in many circumstances but not a sufficient protection against data loss without physical backups, because logical backup provides only structural information.

Importance of Backups

- Planning and testing backup helps against failure of media, operating system, software and any other kind of failures that cause a serious data crash.
- It determines the speed and success of the recovery.
- Physical backup extracts data from physical storage (usually from disk to tape). Operating system is an example of physical backup.
- Logical backup extracts data using SQL from the database and store it in a binary file.
- Logical backup is used to restore the database objects into the database. So the logical backup utilities allow DBA (Database Administrator) to back up and recover selected objects within the database.

Storage of Data

Data storage is the memory structure in the system.

The storage of data is divided into three categories:

- Volatile Memory
- Non – Volatile Memory
- Stable Memory

Volatile Memory

- Volatile memory can store only a small amount of data. For eg. Main memory, cache memory etc.
- Volatile memory is the primary memory device in the system and placed along with the CPU.
- In volatile memory, if the system crashes, then the data will be lost.
- RAM is a primary storage device which stores a disk buffer, active logs and other related data of a database.
- Primary memory is always faster than secondary memory.
- When we fire a query, the database fetches a data from the primary memory and then moves to the secondary memory to fetch the record.
- If the primary memory crashes, then the whole data in the primary memory is lost and cannot be recovered.
- To avoid data loss, create a copy of primary memory in the database with all the logs and buffers, create checkpoints at several places so the data is copied to the database.

Non-Volatile Memory

- Non – volatile memory is the secondary memory.
- These memories are huge in size, but slow in processing. For eg. Flash memory, hard disk, magnetic tapes etc.
- If the secondary memory crashes, whole data in the primary memory is lost and cannot be recovered.

To Avoid Data Loss in the Secondary Memory, There are Three Methods Used to Backup

- **Remote backup** creates a database copy and stores it in the remote network. The database is updated with the current database and sync with data and other details. The remote backup is also called as an offline backup because it can be updated manually. If the current database fails, then the system automatically switches to the remote database and starts functioning. The user will not know that there was a failure.

- The database is copied to secondary memory devices like Flash memory, hard disk, magnetic tapes, etc. and kept in a secured place. If the system crashes or any failure occurs, the data would be copied from these tapes to bring the database up.
- The huge amount of data is an overhead to back up the whole database. To overcome this problem the log files are backed up at regular intervals. The log file includes all the information about the transaction being made. These files are backed up at regular intervals and the database is backed up once in a week.

Stable Memory

- Stable memory is the third form of the memory structure and same as non-volatile memory.
- In stable memory, copies of the same non – volatile memories are stored in different places, because if the system crashes and data loss occurs, the data can be recovered from other copies.

Causes of Database Failures

- A database includes a huge amount of data and transaction.
- If the system crashes or failure occurs, then it is very difficult to recover the database.

There are some Common Causes of Failures Such As

- System Crash
- Transaction Failure
- Network Failure
- Disk Failure
- Media Failure

Each transaction has ACID property. If we fail to maintain the ACID properties, it is the failure of the database system.

1. System Crash

- System crash occurs when there is a hardware or software failure or external factors like a power failure.

- The data in the secondary memory is not affected when system crashes because the database has lots of integrity. Checkpoint prevents the loss of data from secondary memory.

2. Transaction Failure

- The transaction failure is affected on only few tables or processes because of logical errors in the code.
- This failure occurs when there are system errors like deadlock or unavailability of system resources to execute the transaction.

3. Network Failure

- A network failure occurs when a client – server configuration or distributed database system are connected by communication networks.

4. Disk Failure

- Disk Failure occurs when there are issues with hard disks like formation of bad sectors, disk head crash, unavailability of disk etc.

5. Media Failure

- Media failure is the most dangerous failure because, it takes more time to recover than any other kind of failures.
- A disk controller or disk head crash is a typical example of media failure.
- Natural disasters like floods, earthquakes, power failures, etc. damage the data.

What is Recovery?

- Recovery is the process of restoring a database to the correct state in the event of a failure.
- It ensures that the database is reliable and remains in consistent state in case of a failure.

Database Recovery can be Classified into Two Parts

- **Rolling Forward** applies redo records to the corresponding data blocks.
- **Rolling Back** applies rollback segments to the data files. It is stored in transaction tables.
- We can recover the database using Log–Based Recovery.

Log-based Recovery

- Logs are the sequence of records, that maintain the records of actions performed by a transaction.
- In Log – Based Recovery, log of each transaction is maintained in some stable storage. If any failure occurs, it can be recovered from there to recover the database.
- The log contains the information about the transaction being executed, values that have been modified and transaction state.
- All these information will be stored in the order of execution.

Example: Assume a transaction to modify the address of an employee. The following logs are written for this transaction.

Log 1: Transaction is initiated, writes 'START' log.

Log: $\langle T_n$ START$\rangle$

Log 2: Transaction modifies the address from 'Pune' to 'Mumbai'.

Log: $\langle T_n$ Address, 'Pune', 'Mumbai'$\rangle$

Log 3: Transaction is completed. The log indicates the end of the transaction.

Log: $\langle T_n$ COMMIT$\rangle$

There are two methods of creating the log files and updating the database:

- Deferred Database Modification
- Immediate Database Modification

In Deferred Database Modification, all the logs for the transaction are created and stored into stable storage system. In the above example, three log records are created and stored it in some storage system; the database will be updated with those steps.

In Immediate Database Modification, after creating each log record, the database is modified for each step of log entry immediately. In the above example, the database is modified at each step of log entry that means after first log entry, transaction will hit the database to fetch the record, then the second log will be entered followed by updating the employee's address, then the third log followed by committing the database changes.

Recovery with Concurrent Transaction

- When two transactions are executed in parallel, the logs are interleaved. It would become difficult for the recovery system to return all logs to a previous point and then start recovering.
- To overcome this situation 'Checkpoint' is used.

Checkpoint

- Checkpoint acts like a benchmark.
- Checkpoints are also called as **Syncpoints or Savepoints.**
- It is a mechanism where all the previous logs are removed from the system and stored permanently in a storage system.
- It declares a point before which the database management system was in consistent state and all the transactions were committed.
- It is a point of synchronization between the database and the transaction log file.
- It involves operations like writing log records in main memory to secondary storage, writing the modified blocks in the database buffers to secondary storage and writing a checkpoint record to the log file.
- The checkpoint record contains the identifiers of all transactions that are active at the time of the checkpoint.

Recovery

- When concurrent transactions crash and recover, the checkpoint is added to the transaction and recovery system recovers the database from failure in following manner:
- Recovery system reads the log files from end to start checkpoint. It can reverse the transaction.
- It maintains undo log and redo log.
- It puts the transaction in the redo log if the recovery system sees a log $<T_n, Commit>$.
- It puts the transaction in undo log if the recovery system sees a log with $<T_n, Start>$.

All the transactions in the undo log are undone and their logs are removed.

All the transactions in the redo log and their previous logs are removed and then redone before saving their logs.

Recovery and Atomicity

When a system crashes, it may have several transactions being executed and various files opened for them to modify the data items. Transactions are made of various operations, which are atomic in nature. But according to ACID properties of DBMS, atomicity of transactions as a whole must be maintained, that is, either all the operations are executed or none.

When a DBMS recovers from a crash, it should maintain the following:

- It should check the states of all the transactions, which were being executed.

- A transaction may be in the middle of some operation; the DBMS must ensure the atomicity of the transaction in this case.

- It should check whether the transaction can be completed now or it needs to be rolled back.

- No transactions would be allowed to leave the DBMS in an inconsistent state.

There are two types of techniques, which can help a DBMS in recovering as well as maintaining the atomicity of a transaction:

- Maintaining the logs of each transaction, and writing them onto some stable storage before actually modifying the database.

- Maintaining shadow paging, where the changes are done on a volatile memory, and later, the actual database is updated.

Log-based Recovery

Log is a sequence of records, which maintains the records of actions performed by a transaction. It is important that the logs are written prior to the actual modification and stored on a stable storage media, which is failsafe.

Log-based recovery works as follows:

- The log file is kept on a stable storage media.

- When a transaction enters the system and starts execution, it writes a log about it.

$$<T_n, Start>$$

When the transaction modifies an item X, it write logs as follows:

$$<T_n, X, V_1, V_2>$$

It reads T_n has changed the value of X, from V_1 to V_2.

When the transaction finishes, it logs:

$$<T_n, commit>$$

The database can be modified using two approaches:

- **Deferred database modification:** All logs are written on to the stable storage and the database is updated when a transaction commits.

- **Immediate database modification:** Each log follows an actual database modification. That is, the database is modified immediately after every operation.

Recovery with Concurrent Transactions

When more than one transaction are being executed in parallel, the logs are interleaved. At the time of recovery, it would become hard for the recovery system to backtrack all logs, and then start recovering. To ease this situation, most modern DBMS use the concept of 'checkpoints'.

Checkpoint

Keeping and maintaining logs in real time and in real environment may fill out all the memory space available in the system. As time passes, the log file may grow too big to be handled at all. Checkpoint is a mechanism where all the previous logs are removed from the system and stored permanently in a storage disk. Checkpoint declares a point before which the DBMS was in consistent state, and all the transactions were committed.

Recovery

When a system with concurrent transactions crashes and recovers, it behaves in the following manner:

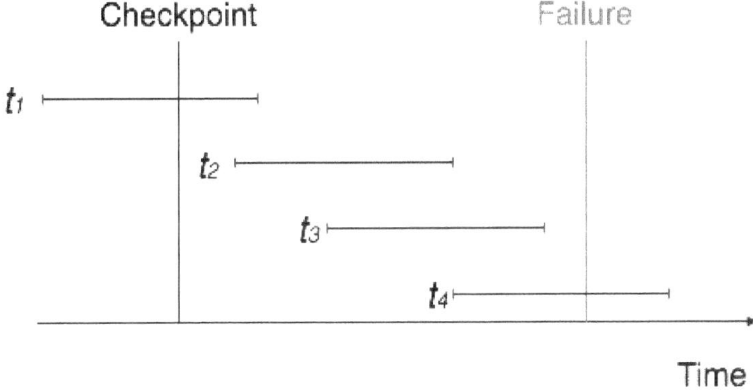

- The recovery system reads the logs backwards from the end to the last checkpoint.
- It maintains two lists, an undo-list and a redo-list.
- If the recovery system sees a log with $<T_n, Start>$ and $<T_n, Commit>$ or just $<T_n, Commit>$, it puts the transaction in the redo-list.
- If the recovery system sees a log with $<T_n, Start>$ but no commit or abort log found, it puts the transaction in undo-list.

All the transactions in the undo-list are then undone and their logs are removed. All the transactions in the redo-list and their previous logs are removed and then redone before saving their logs.

Failure with Loss of Nonvolatile Storage

- So far we assumed no loss of non-volatile storage.
- Technique similar to check pointing used to deal with loss of nonvolatile storage.
- Periodically dump the entire content of the database to stable storage.
- No transaction may be active during the dump procedure; a procedure similar to check pointing must take place.
- Output all log records currently residing in main memory onto stable storage.
- Output all buffer blocks onto the disk.
- Copy the contents of the database to stable storage.
- Output a record to log on stable storage.

Recovering from Failure of Non-Volatile Storage Volatile Storage

- To recover from disk failure z restore database from most recent dump.
- Consult the log and redo all transactions that committed after the dump.
- Can be extended to allow transactions to be active during dump; known as fuzzy dump or online dump.
- Will study fuzzy check pointing later.

Database Buffering

- Database maintains an in-memory buffer of data blocks.
- When a new block is needed, if buffer is full an existing block needs to be removed from buffer If the block chosen for removal has been updated, it must be output to disk.
- If a block with uncommitted updates is output to disk, log records with undo information for the updates are output to the log on stable storage first (Write ahead logging).
- No updates should be in progress on a block when it is output to disk.
- Can be ensured as follows.
- Before writing a data item, transaction acquires exclusive lock on block containing the data item Lock can be released once the write is completed.

- Such locks held for short duration are called latches.

- Before a block is output to disk, the system acquires an exclusive latch on the block.

- Ensures no update can be in progress on the block.

- Database buffer can be implemented either in an area of real main-memory reserved for the database, or in virtual memory.

Implementing buffer in reserved main-memory has drawbacks:

- Memory is partitioned before-hand between database buffer and applications, limiting flexibility.

- Needs may change, and although operating system knows best how memory should be divided up at any time, it cannot change the partitioning of memory.

Database buffers are generally implemented in virtual memory in spite of some drawbacks:

- When operating system needs to evict a page that has been modified, the page is written to swap space on disk.

- When database decides to write buffer page to disk, buffer page may be in swap space, and may have to be read from swap space on disk and output to the database on disk, resulting in extra I/O! Known as dual paging problem.

- Ideally when OS needs to evict a page from the buffer, it should pass control to database, which in turn should.

  - Output the page to database instead of to swap space (making sure to output log records first), if it is modified.

  - Release the page from the buffer, for the OS to use Dual paging can thus be avoided, but common operating systems do not support such functionality.

Advanced Recovery Algorithm

Support for high-concurrency locking techniques, such as those used for B[+]-tree concurrency control, which release locks early.

Supports "logical undo".

Recovery based on "repeating history", whereby recovery executes exactly the same actions as normal processing including redo of log records of incomplete transactions, followed by subsequent undo.

Key Benefits

- Supports logical undo.
- Easier to understand/show correctness.

4.5.   Early Lock Release and Logical Undo Operations

Advanced Recovery: Logical Undo Logging

- Operations like B+-tree insertions and deletions release locks early.
- They cannot be undone by restoring old values (physical undo), since once a lock is released, other transactions may have updated the B+-tree.
- Instead, insertions (resp. deletions) are undone by executing a deletion (resp. insertion) operation (known as logical undo).
- For such operations, undo log records should contain the undo operation to be executed.
- Such logging is called logical undo logging, in contrast to physical undo logging.
- Operations are called logical operations.

Other Examples

- Delete of tuple, to undo insert of tuple.
  - Allows early lock release on space allocation information.
- Subtract amount deposited, to undo deposit.
  - Allows early lock release on bank balance.

Advanced Recovery: Physical Redo

- Redo information is logged physically (that is, new value for each write) even for operations with logical undo.
- Logical redo is very complicated since database state on disk may not be "operation consistent" when recovery starts.
- Physical redo logging does not conflict with early lock release.

Advanced Recovery: Operation Logging

Operation logging is done as follows:

- When operation starts, log $<T_i, O_j,$ operation-begin>. Here O_j is a unique identifier of the operation instance.

- While operation is executing, normal log records with physical redo and physical undo information are logged.

- When operation completes, $<T_i, O_j,$ operation-end, $U>$ is logged, where U contains information needed to perform a logical undo information.

Example: insert of (key, record-id) pair (K5, RID7) into index I9.

```
<T1, O1, operation-begin>

....

<T1, X, 10, K5>
<T1, Y, 45, RID7>
<T1, O1, operation-end, (delete I9, K5, RID7)>
```

If crash/rollback occurs before operation completes:

- The operation-end log record is not found.

- The physical undo information is used to undo operation.

If crash/rollback occurs after the operation completes:

- The operation-end log record is found, and in this case.

- Logical undo is performed using U; the physical undo information for the operation is ignored.

4.6. Redo of Operation (After Crash) Still Uses Physical Redo Information

Advanced Recovery: Transaction Rollback

Rollback of transaction T_i is done as follows:

Scan the log backwards.

- If a log record $<T_i, X, V_1, V_2>$ is found, perform the undo and log a special redo-only log record $<T_i, X, V_1>$.

- If a $<T_i, O_j,$ operation-end, $U>$ record is found.

  - Rollback the operation logically using the undo information U.

    - Updates performed during roll back are logged just like during normal operation execution.

    - At the end of the operation rollback, instead of logging an operation-end record, generate a record.

- $<T_i, O_j,$ operation-abort>.

    - Skip all preceding log records for T_i until the record.

        - $<T_i, O_j$ operation-begin> is found.

Scan the log backwards (cont.):

- If a redo-only record is found ignore it.

- If a $<T_i, O_j,$ operation-abort> record is found:

    - skip all preceding log records for T_i until the record.

        - $<T_i, O_j,$ operation-begin> is found.

- Stop the scan when the record $<T_i,$ start> is found.

- Add a $<T_i,$ abort> record to the log.

Some Points to Note

Cases 3 and 4 above can occur only if the database crashes while a transaction is being rolled back.

Skipping of log records as in case 4 is important to prevent multiple rollback of the same operation.

Remote Backup Systems

Remote backup systems provide high availability by allowing transaction processing to continue even if the primary site is destroyed.

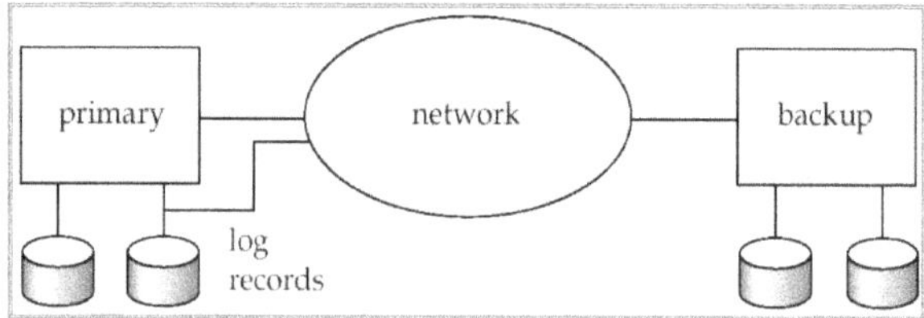

Detection of Failure

Backup site must detect when primary site has failed to distinguish primary site failure from link failure maintain several communication links between the primary and the remote backup. Heart-beat messages.

Transfer of control: To take over control backup site first perform recovery using its copy of the database and all the long records it has received from the primary.

Thus, completed transactions are redone and incomplete transactions are rolled back.

When the backup site takes over processing it becomes the new primary.

To transfer control back to old primary when it recovers, old primary must receive redo logs from the old backup and apply all updates locally.

Time to recover: To reduce delay in takeover, backup site periodically processes the redo log records (in effect, performing recovery from previous database state), performs a checkpoint, and can then delete earlier parts of the log.

Hot-Spare configuration permits very fast takeover: Backup continually processes redo log record as they arrive, applying the updates locally.

When failure of the primary is detected the backup rolls back incomplete transactions, and is ready to process new transactions.

Alternative to remote backup: distributed database with replicated data z Remote backup is faster and cheaper, but less tolerant to failure.

Ensure durability of updates by delaying transaction commit until update is logged at backup; avoid this delay by permitting lower degrees of durability.

One-safe: commit as soon as transaction's commit log record is written at primary Problem: updates may not arrive at backup before it takes over.

Two-very-safe: commit when transaction's commit log record is written at primary and backup z Reduces availability since transactions cannot commit if either site fails.

Two-safe: proceed as in two-very-safe if both primary and backup are active. If only the primary is active, the transaction commits as soon as is commit log record is written at the primary. Better availability than two-very-safe; avoids problem of lost transactions in one-safe.

5. Storage and Indexing

5.1. Overview of Storage and Indexing

- DB design using logical models (ER/Relational).
    - Appropriate level for designers to begin with.
    - Provide independence from implementation details.
- Performance: another major factor in user satisfaction.
    - Depends on,
        - Efficient data structures for data representation.
        - Efficiency of system operation on those structures.
    - Disks contains data files and system files including dictionary and index files.
- Disk access: one of the most critical factor in performance.

5.2. Data on External Storage

- **Disks:** Can retrieve random pages at (almost) fixed cost but reading several consecutive pages is much faster than reading them in random order.
- **Tapes:** Can only read pages in sequence, Slower but cheaper than disks; used for archival storage.
- **Page:** Unit of information read from or written to disk Size of page: DBMS parameter, 4KB, 8KB.

Disk Space Manager

- Abstraction: a collection of pages.
- Allocate/de-allocate a page.
- Read/write a page.

Page I/O

- Pages read from disk and pages written to disk.
- Dominant cost of database operation.
- **Buffer manager:** Stages pages from external storage to main memory buffer pool. File and index layers make calls to the buffer manager.
- **File organization:** Method of arranging a file of records on external storage.
    - Record id (rid) is sufficient to physically locate record.

Indexes are data structures that allow us to find the record ids of records with given values in index search key fields.

Storage Hierarchy

- DBMS stores information on some storage medium.
    - Primary storage: can be operated directly by CPU.
    - Secondary storage:
        - Larger capacity, lower cost, slower access.
        - Cannot be operated directly by CPU – must be copied to primary storage.
- Secondary storage has major implications for DBMS design.
    - READ: Transfer data to main memory.
    - WRITE: Transfer data from main memory.
    - Both transfers are high-cost operations, relative to in-memory operations, so must be planned carefully.
- Cost and size.
- Main memory is volatile.
- Typical storage hierarchy:
    - Factors: access speed, cost per unit, reliability.
    - Cache and main memory (RAM) for currently used data: fast but costly.
    - Flash memory: limited number of writes (and slow), non-volatile, disk-substitute in embedded systems.
    - Disk for the main database (secondary storage).
    - Tapes for archiving older versions of the data (tertiary storage).

Disks

- Secondary storage device.
- Data is stored and retrieved in units called *disk blocks* or *pages.*
- Unlike RAM, time to retrieve a disk page varies depending upon location on disk.

Therefore, relative placement of pages on disk has major impact on DBMS performance!

Components of a Disk

- The platters spin.
- The arm assembly is moved in or out to position a head on a desired track. Tracks under heads make a *cylinder* (imaginary!).

- Only one head reads/writes at any one time.

- *Block size* is a multiple of *sector size* (which is fixed).

Accessing a Disk Page

- Time to access (read/write) a disk block:

    - *Seek time* (moving arms to position disk head on track).

    - *Rotational delay* (waiting for block to rotate under head).

    - *Transfer time* (actually moving data to/from disk surface).

- Seek time and rotational delay dominates.

    - Seek time varies from about 1 to 20msec.

    - Rotational delay varies from 0 to 10msec.

    - Transfer rate is less than 1msec per 4KB page.

- Key to lower I/O cost: reduce seek/rotation delays.

Arranging Pages on Disk

- *'Next'* block concept:

    - Blocks on same track, followed by,

    - Blocks on same cylinder, followed by,

    - Blocks on adjacent cylinder.

- Blocks in a file should be arranged sequentially on disk (by `next'), to minimize seek and rotational delay.

- For a sequential scan, *pre-fetching* several pages at a time is a big win!.

RAID

- Redundant Arrays of Independent Disks.

- Disk Array: Arrangement of several disks that gives abstraction of a single, large disk.

- Increase performance and reliability.

- Two main techniques: parallelism and redundancy.

    - Data striping: Data is partitioned; size of a partition is called the striping unit. Partitions are distributed over multiple disks.

    - Redundancy: More disks -> more failures. Redundant information allows reconstruction of data if a disk fails.

- RAID levels: level 0 – level 6.

Disk Space Management

- Lowest layer of DBMS software manages space on disk.
- Higher levels call upon this layer to:
  - Allocate/de-allocate a page.
  - Read/write a page.
- Highly desirable that a request for a sequence of pages to be satisfied by allocating the pages sequentially on disk.

File Organization and Indexing

- The **File** is a collection of records. Using the primary key, we can access the records. The type and frequency of access can be determined by the type of file organization which was used for a given set of records.
- File organization is a logical relationship among various records. This method defines how file records are mapped onto disk blocks.
- File organization is used to describe the way in which the records are stored in terms of blocks, and the blocks are placed on the storage medium.
- The first approach to map the database to the file is to use the several files and store only one fixed length record in any given file. An alternative approach is to structure our files so that we can contain multiple lengths for records.
- Files of fixed length records are easier to implement than the files of variable length records.

Objective of File Organization

- It contains an optimal selection of records, i.e., records can be selected as fast as possible.
- To perform insert, delete or update transaction on the records should be quick and easy.
- The duplicate records cannot be induced as a result of insert, update or delete.
- For the minimal cost of storage, records should be stored efficiently.

Types of File Organization

File organization contains various methods. These particular methods have pros and cons on the basis of access or selection. In the file organization, the programmer decides the best-suited file organization method according to his requirement.

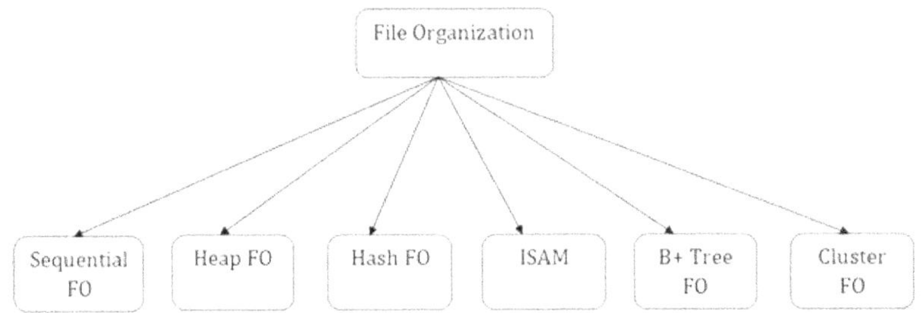

B+ File Organization

- B+ tree file organization is the advanced method of an indexed sequential access method. It uses a tree-like structure to store records in File.

- It uses the same concept of key-index where the primary key is used to sort the records. For each primary key, the value of the index is generated and mapped with the record.

- The B+ tree is similar to a binary search tree (BST), but it can have more than two children. In this method, all the records are stored only at the leaf node. Intermediate nodes act as a pointer to the leaf nodes. They do not contain any records.

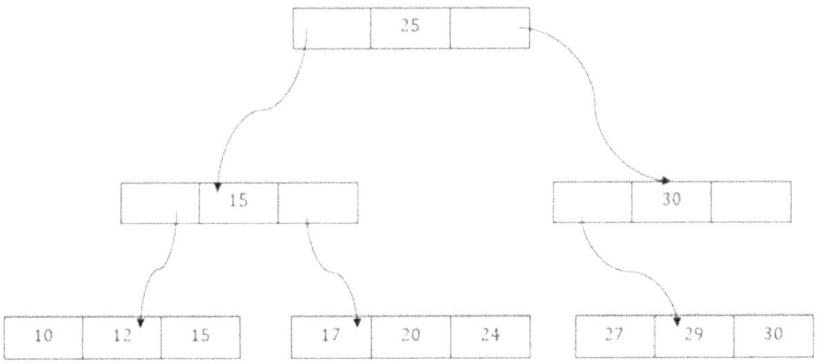

The above B+ Tree Shows That

- There is one root node of the tree, i.e., 25.

- There is an intermediary layer with nodes. They do not store the actual record. They have only pointers to the leaf node.

- The nodes to the left of the root node contain the prior value of the root and nodes to the right contain next value of the root, i.e., 15 and 30 respectively.

- There is only one leaf node which has only values, i.e., 10, 12, 17, 20, 24, 27 and 29.

- Searching for any record is easier as all the leaf nodes are balanced.

- In this method, searching any record can be traversed through the single path and accessed easily.

Pros of B+ Tree File Organization

- In this method, searching becomes very easy as all the records are stored only in the leaf nodes and sorted the sequential linked list.

- Traversing through the tree structure is easier and faster.

- The size of the B+ tree has no restrictions, so the number of records can increase or decrease and the B+ tree structure can also grow or shrink.

- It is a balanced tree structure, and any insert/update/delete does not affect the performance of tree.

Cons of B+ Tree File Organization

- This method is inefficient for the static method.

Index Data Structures

- Indexing is used to optimize the performance of a database by minimizing the number of disk accesses required when a query is processed.

- The index is a type of data structure. It is used to locate and access the data in a database table quickly.

Index Structure

Indexes can be created using some database columns.

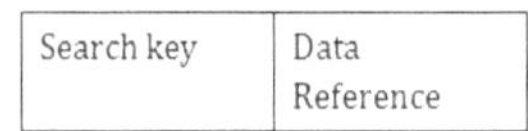

Search key	Data Reference

Fig. Structure of Index

- The first column of the database is the search key that contains a copy of the primary key or candidate key of the table. The values of the primary key are stored in sorted order so that the corresponding data can be accessed easily.

- The second column of the database is the data reference. It contains a set of pointers holding the address of the disk block where the value of the particular key can be found.

Indexing Methods

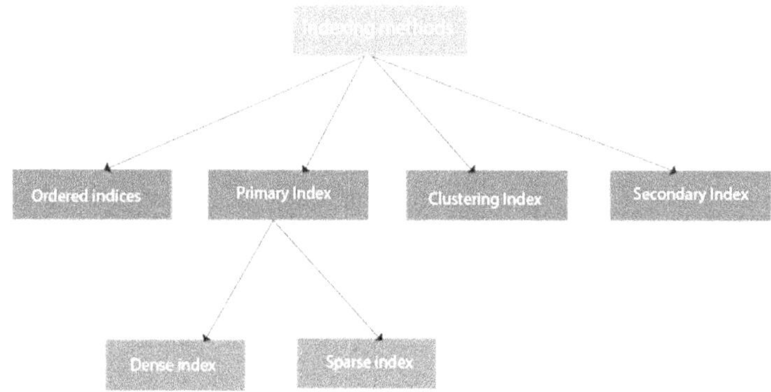

Ordered Indices

The indices are usually sorted to make searching faster. The indices which are sorted are known as ordered indices.

Example: Suppose we have an employee table with thousands of record and each of which is 10 bytes long. If their IDs start with 1, 2, 3.... and so on and we have to search student with ID-543.

- In the case of a database with no index, we have to search the disk block from starting till it reaches 543. The DBMS will read the record after reading 543*10−5430 bytes.
- In the case of an index, we will search using indexes and the DBMS will read the record after reading 542*2= 1084 bytes which are very less compared to the previous case.

Primary Index

- If the index is created on the basis of the primary key of the table, then it is known as primary indexing. These primary keys are unique to each record and contain 1:1 relation between the records.
- As primary keys are stored in sorted order, the performance of the searching operation is quite efficient.
- The primary index can be classified into two types: Dense index and Sparse index.

Dense Index

- The dense index contains an index record for every search key value in the data file. It makes searching faster.

- In this, the number of records in the index table is same as the number of records in the main table.

- It needs more space to store index record itself. The index records have the search key and a pointer to the actual record on the disk.

UP			UP	Agra	1,604,300
USA			USA	Chicago	2,789,378
Nepal			Nepal	Kathmandu	1,456,634
UK			UK	Cambridge	1,360,364

Sparse Index

- In the data file, index record appears only for a few items. Each item points to a block.

- In this, instead of pointing to each record in the main table, the index points to the records in the main table in a gap.

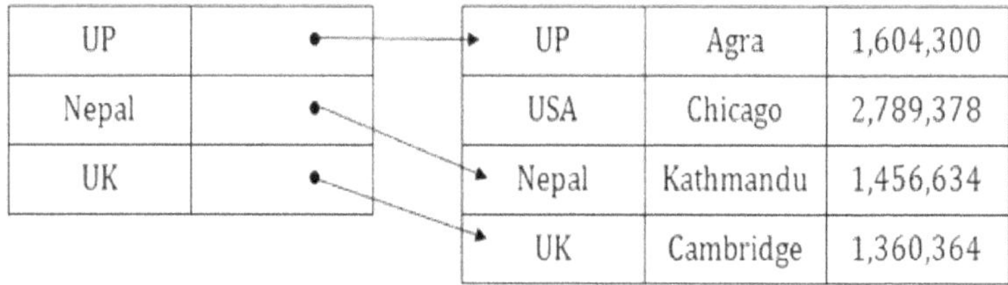

UP			UP	Agra	1,604,300
Nepal			USA	Chicago	2,789,378
UK			Nepal	Kathmandu	1,456,634
			UK	Cambridge	1,360,364

Clustering Index

- A clustered index can be defined as an ordered data file. Sometimes the index is created on non-primary key columns which may not be unique for each record.

- In this case, to identify the record faster, we will group two or more columns to get the unique value and create index out of them. This method is called a clustering index.

- The records which have similar characteristics are grouped, and indexes are created for these group.

Example: Suppose a company contains several employees in each department. Suppose we use a clustering index, where all employees which belong to the same Dept_ID are considered within a single cluster, and index pointers point to the cluster as a whole. Here Dept_Id is a non-unique key.

5.3. Indexed Sequential Access Method (ISAM)

ISAM method is an advanced sequential file organization. In this method, records are stored in the file using the primary key. An index value is generated for each primary key and mapped with the record. This index contains the address of the record in the file.

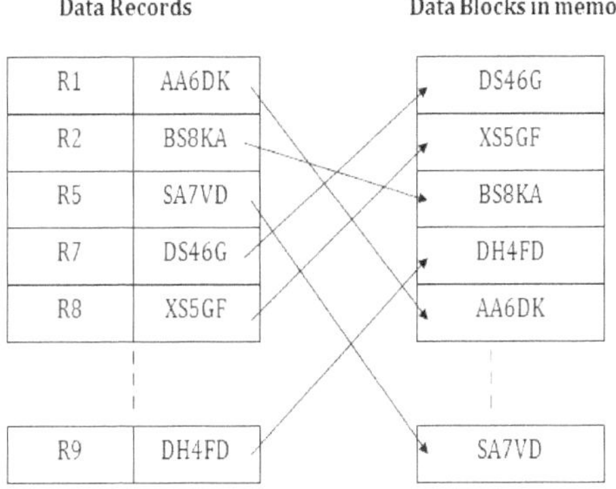

If any record has to be retrieved based on its index value, then the address of the data block is fetched and the record is retrieved from the memory.

Pros of ISAM

- In this method, each record has the address of its data block, searching a record in a huge database is quick and easy.

- This method supports range retrieval and partial retrieval of records. Since the index is based on the primary key values, we can retrieve the data for the given range of value. In the same way, the partial value can also be easily searched, i.e., the student name starting with 'JA' can be easily searched.

Cons of ISAM

- This method requires extra space in the disk to store the index value.

- When the new records are inserted, then these files have to be reconstructed to maintain the sequence.

- When the record is deleted, then the space used by it needs to be released. Otherwise, the performance of the database will slow down.

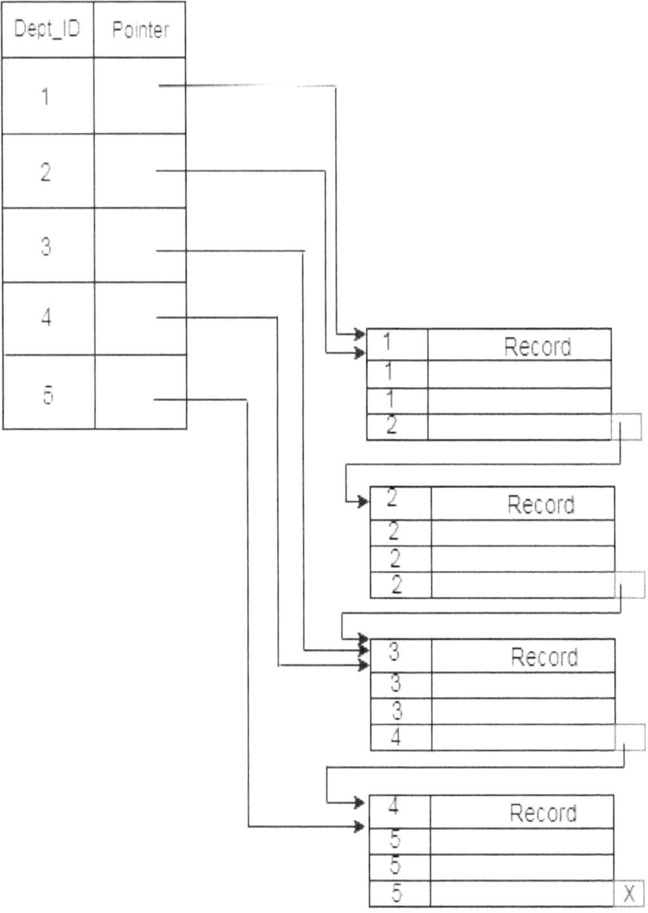

The previous schema is little confusing because one disk block is shared by records which belong to the different cluster. If we use separate disk block for separate clusters, then it is called better technique.

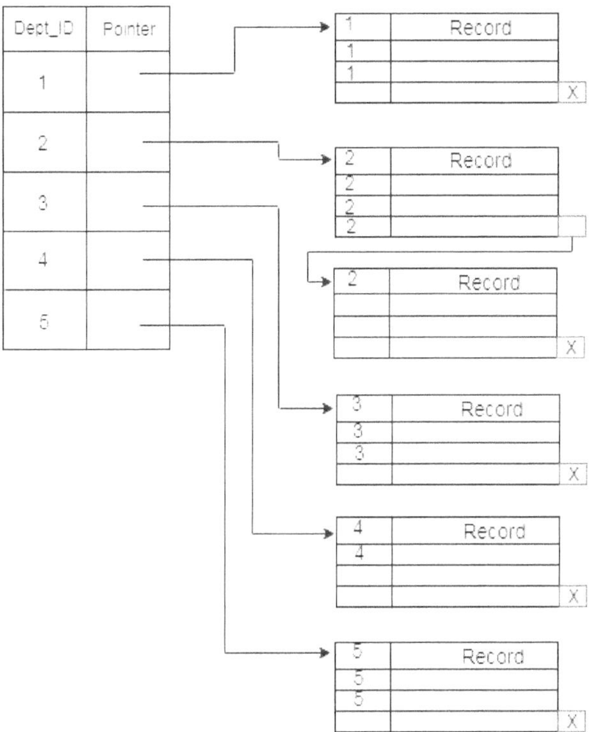

Secondary Index

In the sparse indexing, as the size of the table grows, the size of mapping also grows. These mappings are usually kept in the primary memory so that address fetch should be faster. Then the secondary memory searches the actual data based on the address got from mapping. If the mapping size grows then fetching the address itself becomes slower. In this case, the sparse index will not be efficient. To overcome this problem, secondary indexing is introduced.

In secondary indexing, to reduce the size of mapping, another level of indexing is introduced. In this method, the huge range for the columns is selected initially so that the mapping size of the first level becomes small. Then each range is further divided into smaller ranges. The mapping of the first level is stored in the primary memory, so that address fetch is faster. The mapping of the second level and actual data are stored in the secondary memory (hard disk).

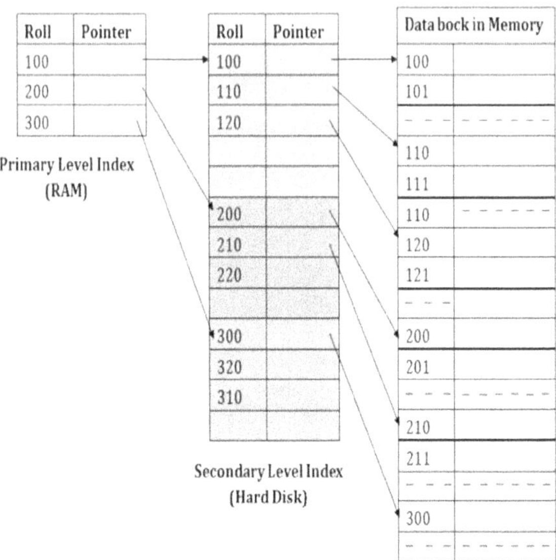

For Example

- If you want to find the record of roll 111 in the diagram, then it will search the highest entry which is smaller than or equal to 111 in the first level index. It will get 100 at this level.

- Then in the second index level, again it does max (111) <= 111 and gets 110. Now using the address 110, it goes to the data block and starts searching each record till it gets 111.

- This is how a search is performed in this method. Inserting, updating or deleting is also done in the same manner.

Hash-based Indexing

Hashing uses hash functions with search keys as parameters to generate the address of a data record.

Hash Organization

- **Bucket:** A hash file stores data in bucket format. Bucket is considered a unit of storage. A bucket typically stores one complete disk block, which in turn can store one or more records.

- **Hash Function:** A hash function, **h,** is a mapping function that maps all the set of search-keys **K** to the address where actual records are placed. It is a function from search keys to bucket addresses.

Static Hashing

In static hashing, when a search-key value is provided, the hash function always computes the same address. For example, if mod-4 hash function is used, then it shall generate only 5 values. The output address shall always be same for that function. The number of buckets provided remains unchanged at all times.

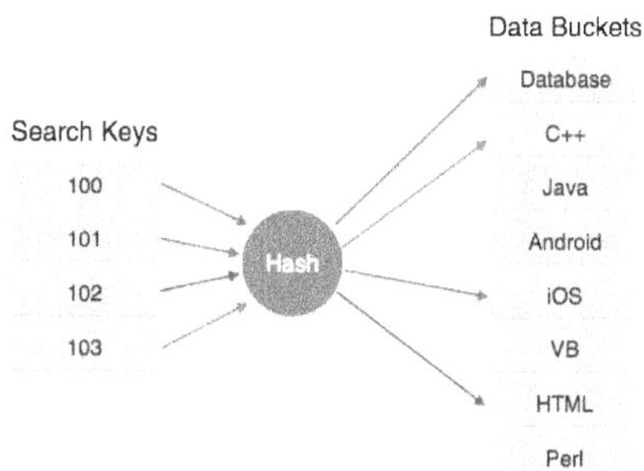

Operation

- **Insertion:** When a record is required to be entered using static hash, the hash function **h** computes the bucket address for search key **K**, where the record will be stored.

$$\text{Bucket address} = h(K)$$

- **Search:** When a record needs to be retrieved, the same hash function can be used to retrieve the address of the bucket where the data is stored.
- **Delete:** This is simply a search followed by a deletion operation.

Bucket Overflow

The condition of bucket-overflow is known as **collision**. This is a fatal state for any static hash function. In this case, overflow chaining can be used.

- **Overflow Chaining:** When buckets are full, a new bucket is allocated for the same hash result and is linked after the previous one. This mechanism is called **Closed Hashing.**

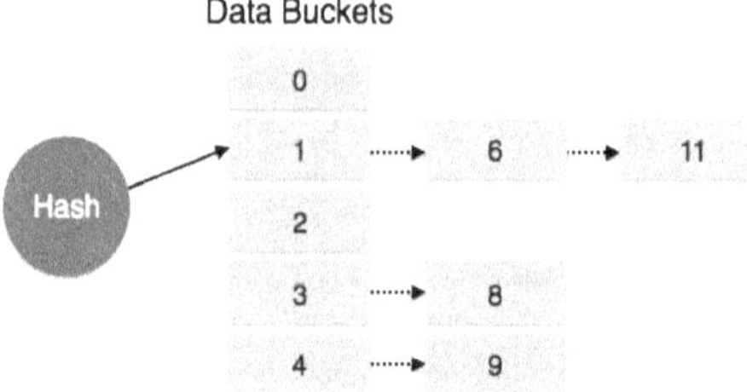

- **Linear Probing:** When a hash function generates an address at which data is already stored, the next free bucket is allocated to it. This mechanism is called **Open Hashing**.

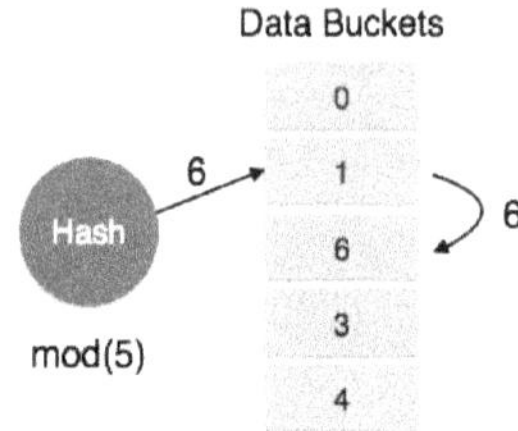

Dynamic Hashing

The problem with static hashing is that it does not expand or shrink dynamically as the size of the database grows or shrinks. Dynamic hashing provides a mechanism in which data buckets are added and removed dynamically and on-demand. Dynamic hashing is also known as **extended hashing.**

Hash function, in dynamic hashing, is made to produce a large number of values and only a few are used initially.

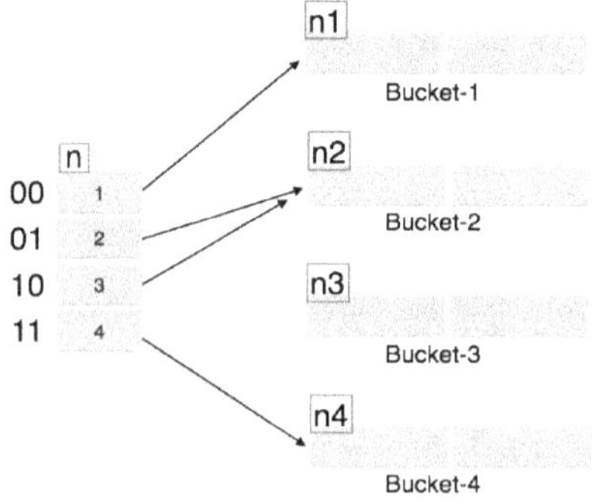

Organization

The prefix of an entire hash value is taken as a hash index. Only a portion of the hash value is used for computing bucket addresses. Every hash index has a depth value to signify how many bits are used for computing a hash function. These bits can address 2n buckets. When all these bits are consumed – that is, when all the buckets are full – then the depth value is increased linearly and twice the buckets are allocated.

Operation

- **Querying:** Look at the depth value of the hash index and use those bits to compute the bucket address.

- **Update:** Perform a query as above and update the data.

- **Deletion:** Perform a query to locate the desired data and delete the same.

- **Insertion:** Compute the address of the bucket.

  - If the bucket is already full.

    - Add more buckets.

    - Add additional bits to the hash value.

    - Re-compute the hash function.

  - Else

    - Add data to the bucket.

  - If all the buckets are full, perform the remedies of static hashing.

Hashing is not favorable when the data is organized in some ordering and the queries require a range of data. When data is discrete and random, hash performs the best

Hashing algorithms have high complexity than indexing. All hash operations are done in constant time.

Linear Hashing

The problem with Extensible Hashing.

Main disadvantage of Extensible Hashing:

- The size of the bucket array will double each time the parameter i increases by 1.
- This exponential growth rate is too fast.

Intro to Linear Hashing (and to Contrast with Extensible Hashing)

Properties of the Linear Hashing technique:

- The growth rate of the bucket array will be linear (hence its name).

- The decision to increase the size of the bucket array is flexible.

A commonly used criterion is:

If (the average occupancy per bucket > some threshold) then:

- Split one bucket into two.

- Linear hashing uses overflow buckets.

Parameters Used in Linear Hashing

- Parameters used in Linear Hashing:

  - n = the number of buckets that is currently in use.

There is also a derived parameter i:

$$i = \lceil \log_2 (n) \rceil$$

The parameter i is the number of bits needed to represent a bucket index in binary:

#buckets bucket indexes

n used i = $\lceil \log(n) \rceil$

```
--------------------------------------------------
1    0                    1 bit // 1 bucket --> bucket 0
2    0 1                  1 bit // 2 buckets --> bucket 0 and 1
3    00 01 10             2 bits
4    00 01 10 11          2 bits
5    000 001... 100       3 bits
6    000 001... 101       3 bits
7    000 001... 110       3 bits
8    000 001... 111       3 bits
9    0000 0001... 1000    4 bits
....
```

The n buckets are number as:

$$0, 1, 2,...., (n{-}1) \; // \text{ In binary}$$

Important Property

When the number (n – 1) is written as i bits binary number:

The first bit in the binary number is always "1".

Example

```
n     n-1 in binary i = ⌈log(n)⌉
-------------------------------------------
2    1 1         1 bits
3    2 10        2 bits
4    3 11        2 bits
5    4 100       3 bits
6    5 101       3 bits
7    6 110       3 bits
8    7 111       3 bits
...  ^
     ¦
First bit = 1!!
```

Consequently

For any number x: (n – 1) < x < 2i-1:

- When x is written as i bits binary number:

- The first bit in the binary number (for x) is always "1".

Example of Parameters in the Linear Hashing Method

Example:

- n = 2 (2 buckets in use, bucket indexes: 0 .. 1).

- i = 1 (1 bit needed to represent a bucket index).

Suppose the number of records r = 3:

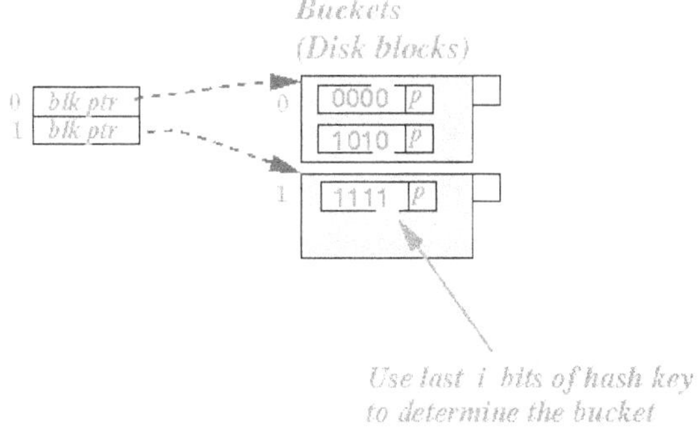

Linear Hashing Technique

- Hash function used in Linear Hashing:

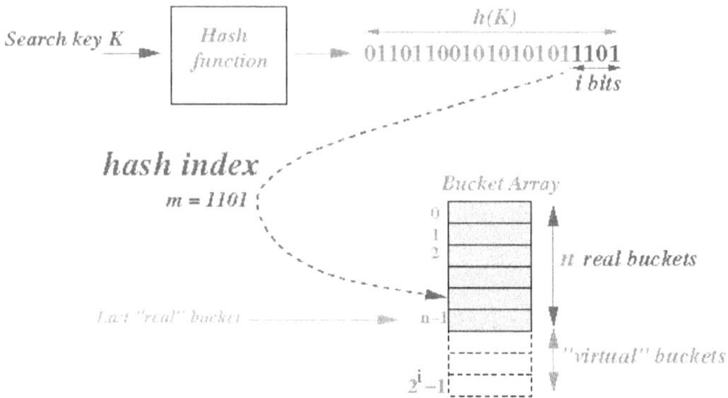

- The bucket index consists of the last i bits in the hash function value.

A bucket in Linear Hashing is a chain of disk blocks:

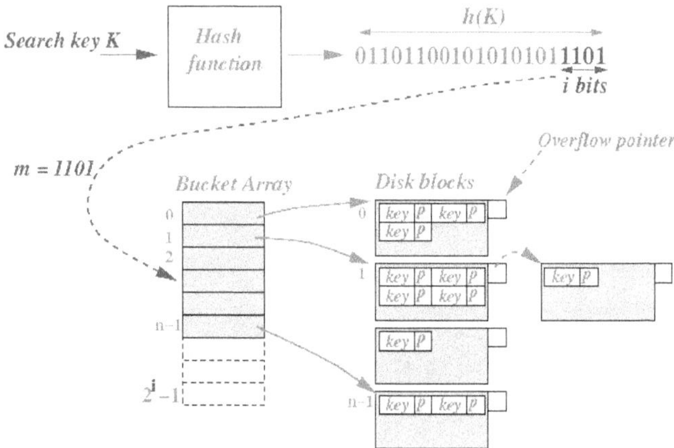

Note: There are only n buckets in use

However:

A hash key value consists of i bits

i.e.: A hash key value can address: 2i buckets!!!

And:

$n \le 2^i$

Therefore:

A hash key value that is > (n – 1) will lead to (what I call) ghost buckets:

"Ghost" bucket = a non-existing bucket!!!

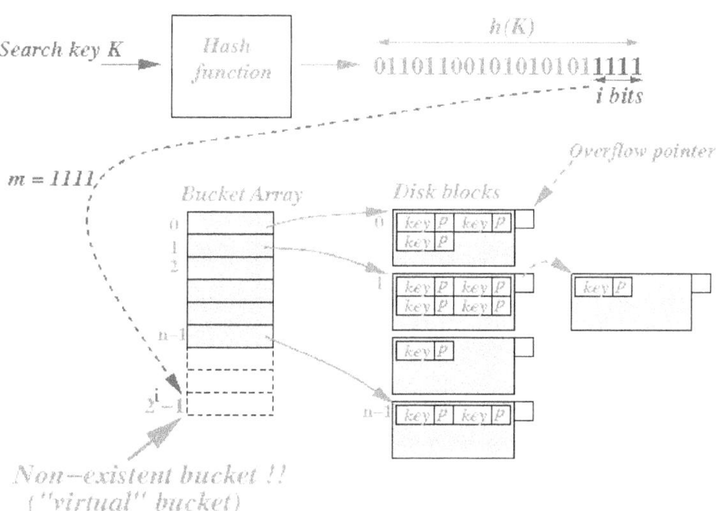

Therefore:

The "ghost" buckets (the non-existent buckets) must have as first bit the binary number 1:

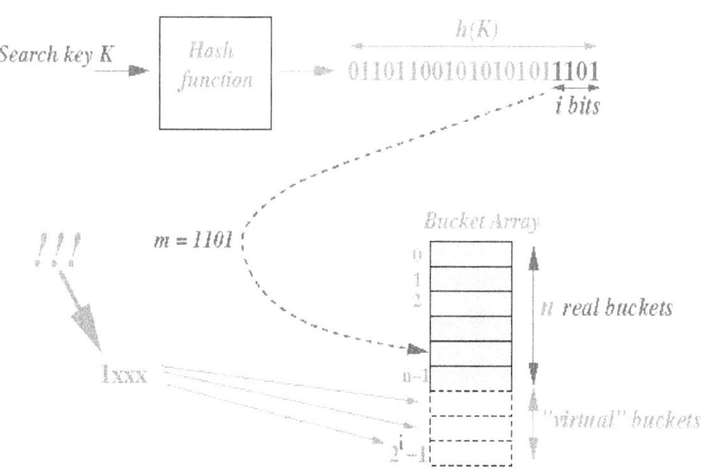

Notice that:

- When we change the first bit of a "ghost" bucket index from 1 to 0:
- The result index identifies a real bucket!!!.
- (Because the last bucket is (n–1) starts with a 1 bit!!!).

5.4. Extendible vs. Linear Hashing

The following factors are used to compare the linear hashing and the extendible hashing schemes.

- **Average Space Utilization:** Divide the current number of records in all the buckets by the maximum number of records that these buckets can hold. Here the buckets include primary as well as overflow buckets.

- **Number of Buckets:** Number of both primary and overflow buckets used in inserting the records. This factor is tied to average space utilization. The higher the space utilization, the fewer the buckets.

- **Average Unsuccessful Search Cost (in terms of bucket accesses):** Reading a primary or an overflow bucket amounts to 1 bucket access. Hence, add the number of buckets, both primary and overflow, that are accessed to search a non-existent record. Divide that sum by the total number of unsuccessful search operations. The cost for a single unsuccessful search is equal to the number of buckets on a particular chain i.e. 1 for the primary bucket plus 1 for each additional overflow bucket attached to the primary bucket.

- **Average Successful Search Cost (in terms of bucket accesses):** Reading a primary or an overflow bucket amounts to 1 bucket access. Hence, add the number of buckets, both primary and overflow, that are accessed to search an existing record. Divide that sum by the total number of successful search operations. Only 1 access is required to retrieve the record contained in the primary bucket. If the record belongs to the overflow bucket, 2 or more accesses are required.

- **Cost of Expansion:** Expansion cost and split cost is synonymously used. Since the expansion process for both extendible and linear hashing is different, the expansion cost calculations also differ. Extendible Hashing: 1 or more accesses to write the old bucket 39 + 1 or more accesses to write the new bucket + 1 access to update the directory pointer (if directory is on secondary storage) + Accesses to update the directory pointers in case of doubling the directory size (if directory is on secondary storage) Linear Hashing: 1 or more accesses to read the bucket to be split + 1 or more accesses to write the old bucket + 1 or more accesses to write the new bucket.

- **Cost of Insertion:** Cost of insertion is based on the number of accesses needed to insert a new record. Cost of connecting a record to the bucket and cost of allocating a new bucket in case of split are being ignored in our analysis. Such costs are system dependent and stay constant for all the records and the buckets. Further they are identical for both the hashing schemes. Cost of insertion consists of unsuccessful search cost and cost of expansion in case of split. In case of split, all the records contained in the bucket have to be redistributed between the old bucket and the newly allocated bucket. In linear hashing, 1 extra access is required to update the next pointer if the last bucket on the chain is full.

- **Size of the Overflow Area:** Count the overflow buckets chained with the primary buckets. (40).

- **CPU time for insertion:** System dependent functions are used to derive the CPU time for inserting the keys.